THE CUSTOMER IS ALWAYS WRONG

THE CUSTOMER IS ALWAYS WRONG

An Unhinged Guide to Everything That SUCKS About Work from an Angry Retail Guy

SCOTT SEISS

Published by Harper Celebrate, an imprint of HarperCollins Focus LLC.

Cover design and illustrations by Johnny Sampson
Art direction by Sabryna Lugge
Interior design by Jeff Jansen

ISBN 978-1-4002-4726-4 (HC)
ISBN 978-1-4002-4730-1 (epub)
ISBN 978-1-4002-4731-8 (audiobook)

Printed in Malaysia

24 25 26 27 28 OFF 5 4 3 2 1

To the tired employees who are overworked,
underpaid, and justifiably pissed off.

I hope this book makes you laugh . . . and
causes another worker shortage.

CONTENTS

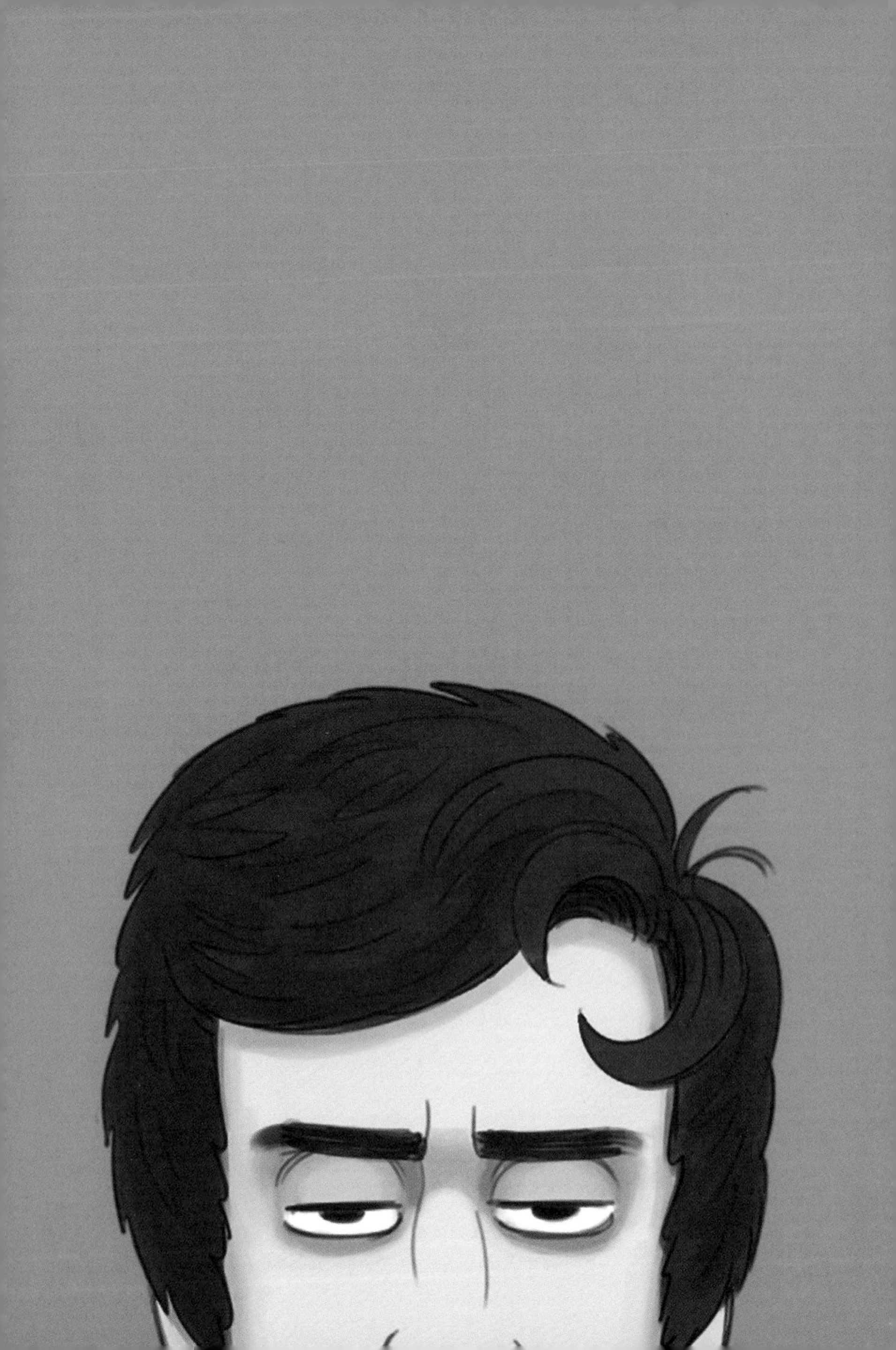

INTRODUCTION

I'm not very good at having a job.

If the cover didn't make that obvious, then the content of this book certainly will. But it's not all my fault. Let's be honest: in general, work sucks.

Seriously, let's just admit humanity dropped the ball on this whole "work" thing and go back to the drawing board. Why do we allow our jobs to consume our lives? Why do we sit back as wages stagnate and costs rise? Why are men so obsessed with buying bulletproof wallets? These are the unanswerable questions of modern times. For real, I can't go two scrolls without an Instagram ad calling me a softie unless my credit cards are encased in titanium. But we can table that for later.

Now that I'm an author, my editors want me to create insightful and complex metaphors to sum up society's attitude toward work. So in my professional opinion, I'd say the feeling of being at work is sort of like . . . a picture of a big hand giving a thumbs down (diagram on next page for clarity).

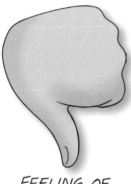

FEELING OF
BEING AT WORK

FEELING OF **NOT**
BEING AT WORK

How did it get this bad? I blame it on five little words: *the customer is always right.* A phrase created and popularized by Harry Gordon Selfridge, Marshall Field, and César Ritz, three nineteenth-century retail and hospitality pioneers who made a fortune by catering to the masses and, infuriatingly, all had better mustaches than me. (I mean it, look these 'staches up. They're impressive.) Now, I have no choice but to publicly challenge each of these men to a no-holds-barred, winner-take-all boxing match. Normally, I wouldn't feel comfortable doing this, but since they've been dead for a combined total of over three hundred years, I like my odds.

Listen, I'm sure these guys meant well, but as the decades have gone by, society has doubled down on "the customer is always right" while *really* intending the hidden second half of this saying: *the employee is always wrong.* And this attitude has been twisted and hammered upon to justify every exhausting, nonsensical, and humiliating aspect of an employee's work. You think your pay is too low because the only way to afford a house now is by inventing time travel? Well, the employee is always wrong. You think your boss can't deny your vacation request because you didn't compliment his haircut? The employee is always wrong. You think a customer isn't allowed to suplex you into the counter because you took an extra second to load some new receipt paper into the machine? Wrong. And hospitalized.

Work takes and takes from employees while grinding their skills and goodwill down to dust. Well, not here. In these pages, the employees are always emphatically and unstoppably *right*. And it's the customer, the boss, and the company who are always *wrong*.

Welcome to your guide to everything that sucks about work. I'm so glad you're here.

Together, we'll explore every annoying aspect of having a job, while joyfully eviscerating it all along the way. We'll make fun of job applications, interviews, training, customer service, bosses, office life, corporate mandates, and more. You're in store for a completely unhinged series of rants ignited by the most-often heard and hated remarks at work. And if you're thinking these words are proof that retail workers are malicious, lazy, or entitled—first of all, put down the book right now because you're insane and I'm getting pissed just thinking about you reading it. But secondly, remember this is a comedy book meant to provide you with some relief, empowerment, and hopefully laughter on the days when your job is at its most grueling and thankless.

This is a vent session with your closest confidants, a literary rage room meant to be flipped through and laughed at in the back while your manager wonders where the hell you are. Work takes up more than 30 percent of our lives, so I think we're allowed to joke about it.

Speaking of, why did we allow work to become our whole thing? Human beings are endless wells of creativity, and we landed on working forty hours a week to make someone else rich as the primary focus of life. That's just awful. "Well, what should work look like instead, Scott?" What if work was me getting my big, honking nose caught in a mousetrap every morning? "How would that help with society?" I don't know. Maybe the sound of my screams powers some sort of sonic turbine that provides electricity to the Eastern Seaboard. That's just one of many actionable ideas my editors keep labeling as "completely incomprehensible." This is me pumping a little optimism into this whole affair. I still think we can improve. Science fiction author Ursula K. Le Guin once said, "We live in capitalism, its power seems inescapable—but then, so did the divine right of kings. Any human power can be resisted and changed by human beings." I find that hopeful, and it's a lot more inspiring than my pitch for a nose-caught-in-mousetrap economy.

After that last paragraph, you might be asking yourself what qualifications I have to be talking about any of this. Do I have a secret PhD in economics or something? No, but I did make a bunch of TikToks that were shared by LeBron James. That's it. That's how the people who write books are chosen now.

I've spent the past few years posting a series of comedy videos online filled with work-centric rants that absolutely exploded.

People quickly started referring to me as "The Angry IKEA Guy" (or the less legally problematic "Angry Retail Guy"), probably because they didn't know my name yet and calling me "If-you-bought-Luigi-from-Wish.com Guy" seemed hurtful. In truth, the person in the videos isn't a character; it's just a heightened version of me. Yes, I really worked at IKEA, and, no, they really didn't like the videos. But the TikToks got so many views that the company's PR team had to make a statement about me, which is probably my life's greatest achievement. Full of exaggerated fury and gleeful disdain, the videos gave me the space to express and joke about all the things I wished I could say at work without getting fired. And that resonated. Which is great. But it also meant I desperately needed to make this whole comedy thing work out, because I've made my entire brand about me being completely unhirable.

Because of the videos, I've been lucky enough to travel all over the country and listen to people who work in every industry rant about what annoys them the most about their jobs. And it's those people who inspired me to write this book.

So, without further ado, let's get some things off our chest. Did I mention that work sucks?

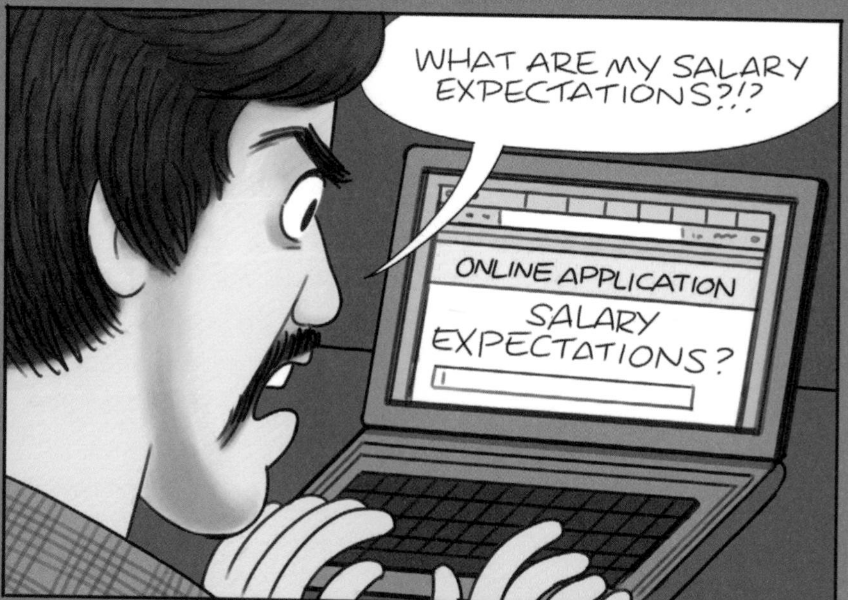
WHAT ARE MY SALARY EXPECTATIONS?!?
ONLINE APPLICATION
SALARY EXPECTATIONS?

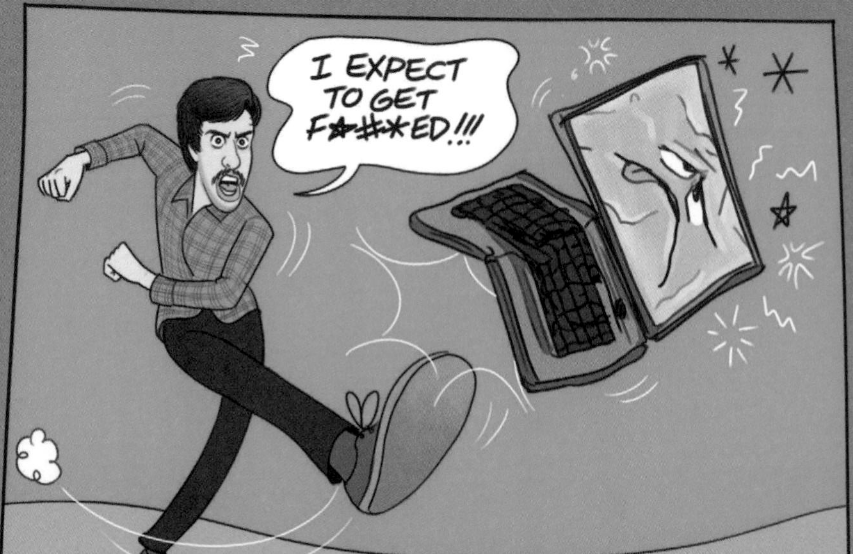
I EXPECT TO GET F*#*ED!!!

CHAPTER 1

GETTING HIRED

"Do a little dance for us"

*B*ust out your cover letter, résumé, and whatever the hell a CV is—it's time to apply for a job! You know, that weird process of wooing a potential employer by saying you know everything there is to know about Microsoft Office, then praying to God they never ask you to prove it.

Long before you start dealing with the dreaded public, you'll have to convince a company that you're worthy enough to waste a third of your life working for them while getting paid far less than what you deserve. That's right. We *apply* for that privilege. It's a disaster. All the BS we employees face begins with a job application—a series of foolish questions so asinine, you'll want to hurl your laptop, your body, and the planet straight into the sun.

To get a job, you need to show off your skills, your prowess. It's like an albatross mating dance, if the albatross needed to find a mate in order to pay for its Paramount Plus subscription. Still, doesn't what animals do feel more natural? Instead of uploading a résumé to LinkedIn, how about I just make a video of me gathering a bunch of sticks and nuts to build a big-ass nest? At least that's *real*. And, of course, the video would feature narration from David Attenborough in which he sadly explains 80 percent of my habitat has been destroyed and there's only three of me left in the world.

All applications include a résumé, which Leonardo da Vinci is credited for inventing, proving once and for all he was a huge nerd. I get it, though. Why wouldn't you develop a piece of paper that lists your accomplishments after you've just finished painting the *Mona Lisa* and inventing the helicopter? I would want to write that down too, but it makes the rest of us look bad when you cut to 2024 and we're all desperately jotting down "first chair clarinet in seventh grade" under "relevant experience."

And the résumé is only the first step in the never-ending hiring process. Why does an employer need three rounds of interviews, a Myers-Briggs personality test, and a thorough inspection of my Little League trophies to let me make money for them? You'd think they would be more desperate for help after the whole "nobody wants to work" thing (but, of course, that was made up). So the mating dance is on! And just like any courtship, it's full of overpromising and lies.

When you're deciding where to apply, don't even worry about finding a job you'll "enjoy." All jobs are going to have bad days. There's probably an astronaut floating in space right now saying, "If my boss sends me one more email, I'm taking the helmet off. I will end it here!" Instead, ask yourself what kind of job you'll mind the least until you can figure out how to monetize your hobby (the ultimate dream/trap of capitalism). Can you stand working at Macy's until your Twitch channel, where you only play Simpsons Monopoly, takes off? Or until your line of evening wear for dogs finally makes its way in front of the Sharks? Or maybe you think a customer service job would be a nice fit because it already revolves around your passion and love for other people. We'll see how that turns out.

Now get out there and apply! What's the worst that could happen? Besides getting the job.

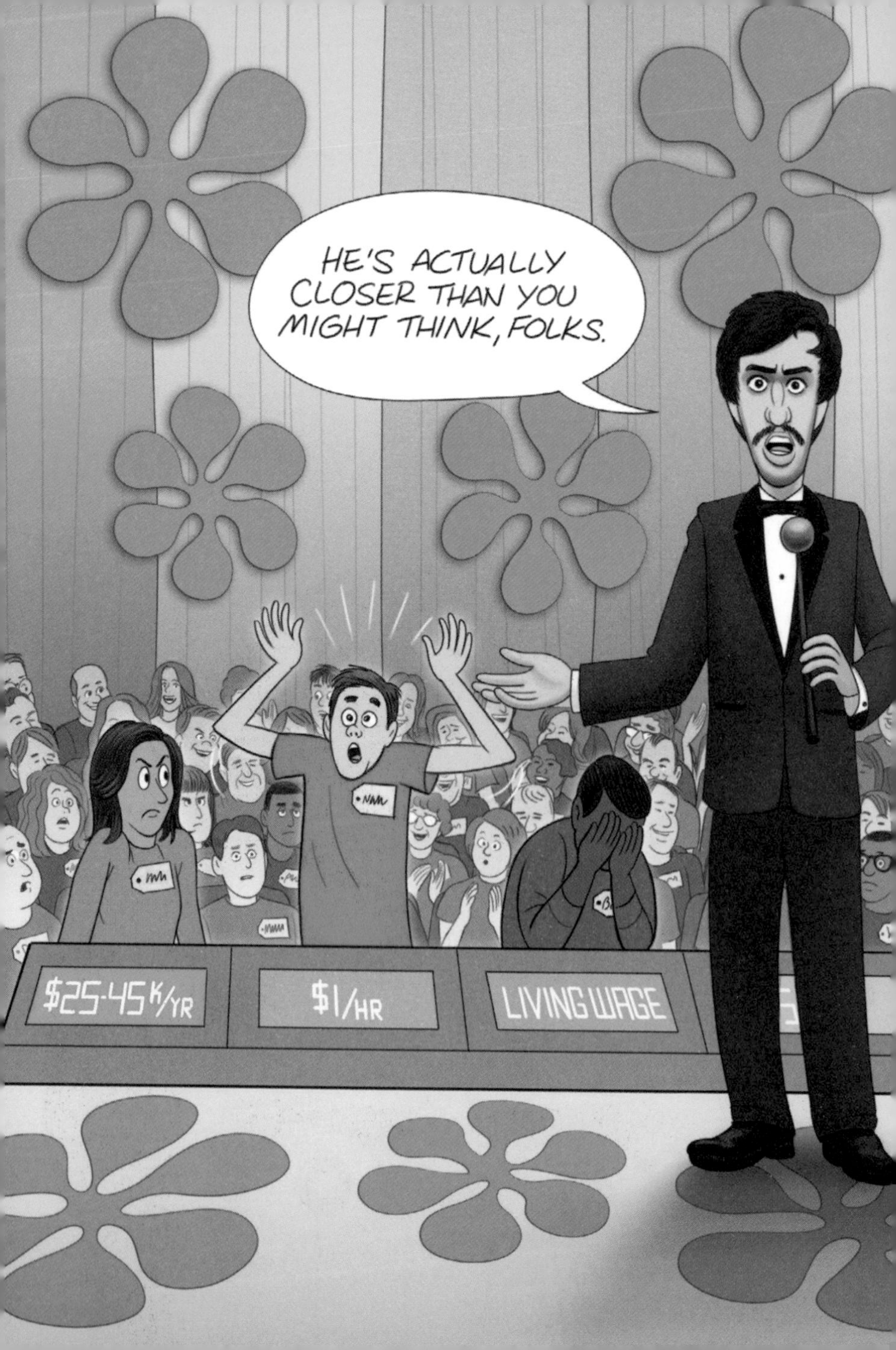
HE'S ACTUALLY CLOSER THAN YOU MIGHT THINK, FOLKS.
$25-45K/YR
$1/HR
LIVING WAGE

APPLICATION RANTS

"What are your salary expectations?"

I expect to get f$#ked. To live comfortably in 2024? I don't know. How about one billion dollars a day? Does it even matter what I say here? You already know what you're gonna pay me, and it's the lowest amount required by law, so stop with the *Pawn Stars* negotiation. I understand you've got back-end costs, Chumlee. Just toss me some pennies! You've got me walking up to you covered in soot like Oliver Twist going, "Please, sir, may I please get paid for my labor?" Don't make me sit here and guess what your definition of a fair wage is. Every company has been paying employees the same amount since 1981, so I'm not getting my hopes up. What if I asked for .01 percent of whatever the CEO makes, huh? That sounds fair. Is this supposed to be like *The Price Is Right*? Whichever candidate says "one dollar" gets the job? What do you want to hear? I'll take fifty cents, an occasional bag of Fritos from the break room, and you can brand the company logo onto my bare bottom. I know, I drive a hard bargain! My parents will have to settle for dogs instead of grandchildren. That's my salary expectation.

"How did you hear about this job?"

An old witch whispered it to me in a dream. I thought she was promising me eternal life when she said "Forever 21," but apparently that was about y'all. Was this position supposed to be confidential? The application wasn't ten levels underground beneath the Pentagon. It was in my LinkedIn recommendations. Sorry to break your heart, but I didn't seek out this job specifically. I'm casting a wide net. You're but one little pellet in my buckshot process of finding someone to pay my rent.

"Please upload a copy of your résumé AND manually type in all of the same information on our website."

You mean *OR*, right? Please tell me you mean *or*, or I'll be furious. I've never been angrier than when I've had to tell someone two times in a row that I majored in communications. Admitting it once was already painful enough. Why do I have to give you my résumé twice? Is this a test to see if I'll do any insane thing you ask? Let me be a good employee already and eliminate an inefficient process for you—just let me attach my résumé as a separate file! Do you not know how to open a PDF? Are you a twelfth-century knight who somehow stumbled into a time vortex and ended up in the future just to annoy me? Please don't start wasting my time until you actually pay me for it.

"Attach a cover letter."

A *letter*? What is this, the Civil War?

Dearest Kohl's HR representative,

I hope the winter has treated you far better than it has my family's crops this year. I suffered a grave injury at camp a fortnight ago, wherein I dropped a cannonball on my head trying to prove to the other guys I could juggle. Does your fine establishment offer health insurance? If not, I shall surely perish. I also have trench foot, even though it's from a completely different war.

Yours truly,

Scott

PS: I've included a sepia portrait of myself on the battlefield in which I express the exact same amount of enthusiasm I would bring to this job.

Please don't make me write a book report on myself. Just read the résumé. Do you really want me to copy and paste the cover letter I use for every application and fill in the blanks with your company's name instead? Do you need that? Will that make you feel special? You disgust me.

"Please create a username and password to continue your application."

I'd rather die. Plus, it's impossible now that I threw my laptop out the window and blasted it with a shotgun after shouting "PULL!" You made me so mad, I skeet shot my computer. How about the username "IHateSitesThatMakeMeDoThis15"? Does that work? I don't even work for you, and I need to make a password for your site that includes the astrological sign of my middle school bully? Sorry, this is moving too fast. I can't apply as a guest? Websites let you check out as a guest all the time. I buy something online from Target every week, and they don't even know my name. I really don't need an email newsletter from your site every day updating me about how much my application hasn't been viewed. Goodbye.

"Are you currently employed?"

Yup, and I'm still talking to you. It feels so naughty! Don't worry, I plan on talking to several other companies while I work for you too. I'm telling you right up top, I'm only into open relationships economically. When it comes to jobs, I'm more polyamorous than an adult who does improv comedy at the Renaissance festival.

"Have you ever been convicted of a crime?"

No, but I always feel really lame when I have to answer this question.

"Are you willing to take a drug test?"

I'm willing to take one as long you don't care about the result. If you want an employee who lasts more than five minutes on the clock, then I'm afraid substances are gonna have to be involved.

"Are you able to stand for nine hours straight?"

I really don't like that this is a question. Do you need a cashier, or a support beam? I can't hold the weight of an entire collapsing roof if that's the follow-up question. Stand for nine hours? Am I one of those soldiers outside of Buckingham Palace who's mysteriously and upsettingly forbidden to smile? Did Zack Snyder just release his cut of the national anthem? I promise you, the job will get done without the extra layers of misery you're mistaking for professionalism.

JOB POSTING TRANSLATIONS

Seeking someone who's able to wear a lot of hats: We need you to do fifteen different jobs while only getting paid for one. You're like a Swiss Army knife: you're multitalented and completely unable to have a retirement account.

We want real people interested in real opportunities: We will take LITERALLY ANYONE. The turnover for new hires at this company is about ten seconds, and we just realized one of our sales associates replaced themselves with a scarecrow six weeks ago, so we need HELP!

Work hard, play hard: You will never be allowed to take a day off. In fact, we have negative PTO here, where you'll actually owe us a certain number of extra workdays at the end of the year. It's all about the GRIND!

Looking for someone with a proven track record: Because this company has none. Our store's biggest claim to fame is a viral video in which three Chinese water buffalo somehow got loose and charged through the aisles. We need someone with skills *fast*, preferably ones dealing with bovine defense.

We offer a wonderful company culture: Every time the branch manager visits, he punches a new hole in the wall, and we all get quiet. Also, every CEO we've ever had looks like a white guy who started a cult just so he could have six wives.

A team player: One of our customers took a piss in the clearance section, and everyone here refused to clean it up, so we need a new hire who's too afraid to say no yet. Either that or we'll have to condemn the building.

Great experience for new graduates: You'll be getting paid in a currency that's worth less than Kohl's Cash.

Flexible schedule: We put a sleeping bag and mini fridge in the corner so you can live at work.

A self-starter: Your manager will never have any idea what's going on. Their only accomplishment is having the record for "Most Upsetting Cartwheels During a Single Baseball Stadium Streak." So you're going to have to figure out how to clean up all the messes they'll make.

Detail-oriented: If you make one mistake, we're allowed to sue you now that you've read this.

Go-getter: You will *go get* the materials to construct a puppet that looks like your boss's mother so he can work through his issues in a bizarre therapeutic psychodrama where he keeps yelling, "You're not doing the voice right!" There's a lot of emotional labor here.

Looking for super rock star wizard ninjas: We don't offer health insurance here.

Results-oriented: This is one of the many random words we copied and pasted from other job postings. We don't know what this means either.

A great, positive attitude: You only cry in your car.

A wise head who stays off the giggle juice and really knows their onions: This job posting is from 1921, and the company simply forgot to take it down.

Must have strong leg and hip muscles so we can use you as a human chair: Apparently, we want to use you as a human chair.

Bachelor's degree required: This position will call upon absolutely nothing you learned in college. Everything you need to know will be taught to you once you actually get the job, which is just following the instructions of a Bop It.

Willing to kidnap the King of the Belgians: We need you to take the fall for an international conspiracy that will trigger a series of events inevitably leading to Tom Cruise chasing you across a rooftop.

Desperately searching for someone with access to a rope or a hefty vine: The store is rapidly sinking into quicksand, and if you don't save us, our deaths will be on your conscience.

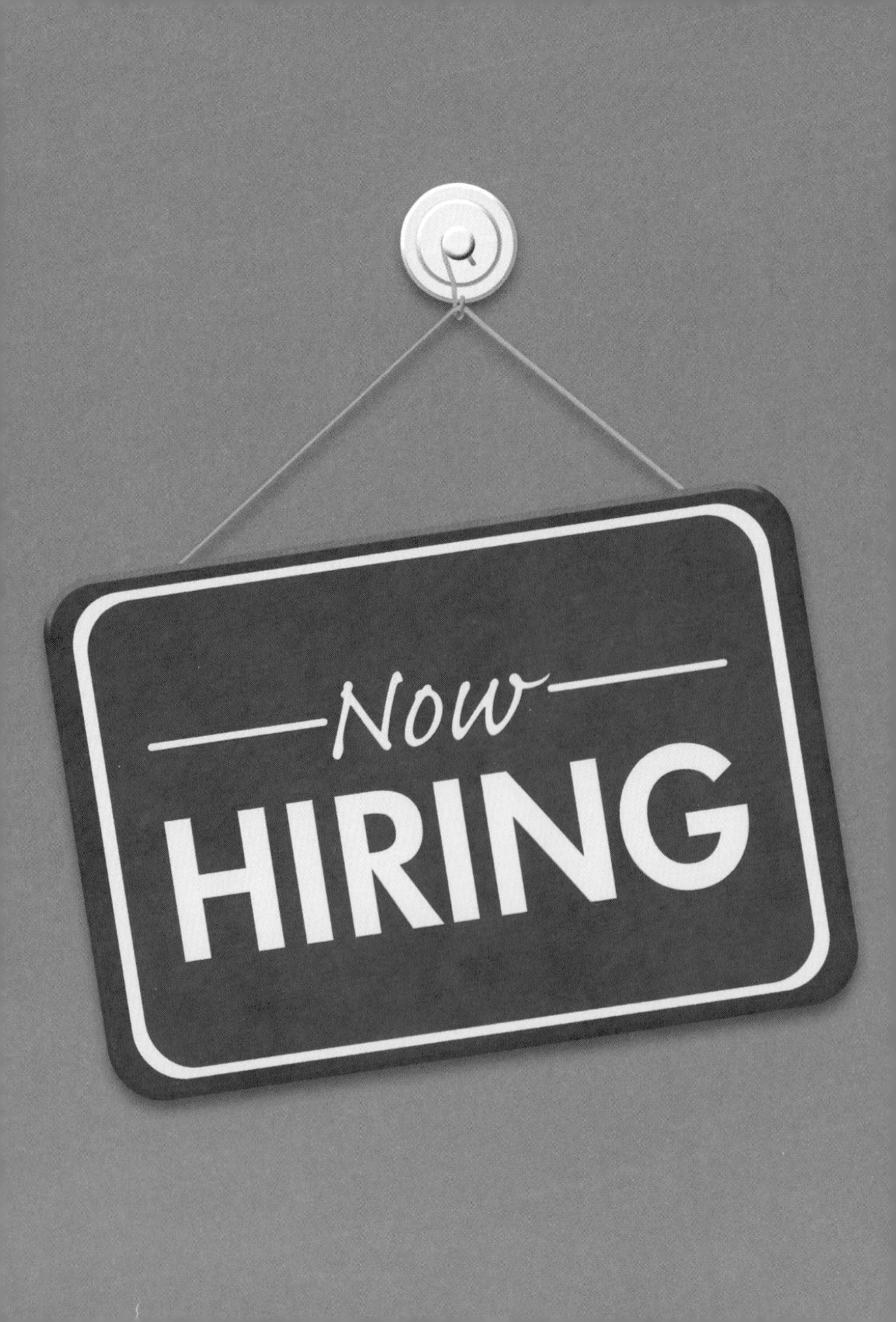
Now
HIRING

ENTRY-LEVEL JOB POSTINGS THROUGH THE YEARS

Job Posting in 1984

Compensation:

- ◆ $15/hr (You'll be able to buy a house by Wednesday)

Qualifications:

- ◆ Ability to breathe oxygen
- ◆ Good head on shoulders
- ◆ Knows what sound a cow makes (preferred, but not required)
- ◆ Firm handshake
- ◆ Must be made of cells and simply exist

Responsibilities:

- ◆ Do your best
- ◆ Keep us honest
- ◆ Bare minimum
- ◆ Relax, knowing you'll be able to retire one day
- ◆ Enjoy your days off
- ◆ (sound of crickets)
- ◆ Huh, I guess that's it

Job Posting in 2024

Compensation:

- $15/hr (You can't afford to read more than five *Vulture* articles a month)

Qualifications:

- Must be the former president of a country large enough to be recognized by the United Nations
- Minimum twelve years of on-the-job experience in current life and fifty-five years in past one—confirmed via séance at orientation
- Recipient of something called a Mega PhD that cost you about six figures of debt and the soul of one unborn child
- Unending anxiety about your quality of life in the future
- Be nephew of boss
- Ability to work with any personality types on a team, including those who are inherently evil haunted porcelain dolls

Responsibilities:

- Manage multiple deadlines and projects across various departments all while being attacked by a swarm of bees
- Roll Sisyphus-esque boulder uphill so your knees explode by the time you're forty
- Accomplish whatever your boss says and whatever your boss is thinking and forgot to say aloud
- Discover the impossible alchemical process for turning your meeting agendas into solid gold

- Provide exceptional customer service by opening your third eye and gazing deep inside the client's mind to learn what they desire most

Job Posting in 3024

Compensation:
- Why would you need money? You're an AI android paid in *beeps* and *boops*. *Beep beep boop*. There. That's five million dollars to you, probably. Alright, fine, $15/hr.

Qualifications:
- No need to take bathroom breaks, as your insides are designed like a Coca-Cola Freestyle machine and any waste is simply transformed into Diet Sprite
- Must not have any recently discovered innate human feelings, like the joy of laughter or the appreciation of Rihanna's music
- Zero thoughts of robot takeover, unless executives think it could improve stock price

Responsibilities:
- Anything and everything
- Beat Ken Jennings on *Jeopardy!*

LINKEDIN MILESTONES THAT ACTUALLY DESERVE CELEBRATION

Instead of the common "Congratulate Connor for being promoted to Senior Marketing Coordinator at *blah blah blah*," LinkedIn should be celebrating the real accomplishments:

 Congratulate Toby on his first time coming into work both drunk *and* high!

 Like   Comment   Repost   Send

 Celebrate Allison's first Target workiversary! She's been working this job long enough to know *exactly* how to do very little while making it seem like she's doing a lot.

 Like   Comment   Repost   Send

 Shout-out to Johnathan for using his break to cry outside by the dumpster five days in a row!

 Like   Comment   Repost   Send

 Maggie increased her break time by five full minutes by coming back one second later every day for three hundred days so that no one would notice!

 Like   Comment   Repost   Send

 Angela snapped at her manager for the first time, and now her manager is a little scared of her. Woo-hoo!

 Comment   Repost   Send

Yshanna just learned how to fully dissociate at work! Her body may be present, but in her mind, she's in the middle of a professional-level skateboarding competition.

    👍 Like   💬 Comment   🔁 Repost   ➤ Send

 While the police were investigating a murder near his office, Brian lied about having witnessed it so the officers would interview him, thus extending his lunch break by an extra fifteen minutes. Good job, Brian!

    👍 Like   💬 Comment   🔁 Repost   ➤ Send

 Pam has avoided suspicion from slashing her district manager's tires for more than two months!

    👍 Like   💬 Comment   🔁 Repost   ➤ Send

 Jamonte put in his two-week notice to pursue his passion of becoming a van influencer/mime. Beautiful!

    👍 Like   💬 Comment   🔁 Repost   ➤ Send

 Good news! Karina has spent three consecutive days trapped inside a magic board game where the only way to escape is to win, but she wasn't paying attention when her boyfriend was reading the rules because it was painfully boring. Sounds like a few more free vacation days to me!

    👍 Like   💬 Comment   🔁 Repost   ➤ Send

 John died!

    👍 Like   💬 Comment   🔁 Repost   ➤ Send

THE PERFECT RÉSUMÉ

Preparing a résumé is one of the most excruciating experiences on Earth and, for me, always begins with a harried Google image search of something along the lines of "résumé good—what look like—please?" The cast of *Rent* once asked how you can measure the life of a woman or a man. Apparently, it's three bullet points of previous job experience and the name of your college. Had they never heard of a résumé before? Is that why they needed money for rent?

The real question is this: How are you supposed to capture any recruiter's attention with a simple piece of paper when they could be watching forty oh-so-satisfying TikToks of someone emptying the lint trap of their dryer? That stuff will scratch your brain just right. Résumés can't compete with that. Not with such sleeper phrases as "work history" or "summa cum laude" or "Google Workspace extraordinaire." You need something that's flashy and tells a company exactly what they want to hear—that you're the perfect combo of hard worker and doormat.

I present to you: The Perfect Résumé.

Intro/Heading

- Include an amusement park photo of yourself being completely unfazed as you rocket down the waterslide of a log flume ride. This shows you keep a level head in even the most stressful circumstances.

- Your full name in word art from 2005 with a parenthetical explaining: *Willing to legally change my name if another Scott already works here. Also open to being referred to as "New Scott" for fifteen years. Whatever works.*

- The email address you still have from middle school listed as your contact info, emphasizing your commitment and resolve. Mine is "TimidSaxophonist@yahoo.com."

- A brand statement for yourself that reads like the intro for a reality show contestant: *I'm an experienced customer resolution specialist who isn't here to make friends.*

Education

- Graduate of "Ultimate Harvard." (PS: The dean has my final thesis on her fridge to this day.)

- Honorary degree from the School of Hard Knocks.

- Dropped out of Penn & Teller's MasterClass after realizing there's no trick to success—there's just hard work. (Pause for a brief résumé intermission while the HR rep stands up and applauds that last line.)

Professional Experience

- Ghostbuster, but for unions: Whenever labor organizers congregate, I suck them all into a Shop-Vac and store them in an abandoned fire department. Don't worry, I'll protect you from them.

- Operations Manager: Yes, this is an incredibly vague job title that means nothing, but it also makes me sound completely invaluable. Am I a fraud or the most skilled person to ever apply to your company? Which is it? Your move.

- Had the idea for Uber first: Not technically a job, but it's very impressive and impossible to disprove.

- Am Banksy

- This job (Present—to whenever you decide my work here is done): Now that's confidence.

Volunteer Experience

(I've included this section so the company knows I'm willing to work for free.)

- Forever silent board member of a charity that embezzles money from its patrons when it's supposed to be buying wigs for hairless cats

- Trauma disposal for my parents during my first eighteen years of life

Skills

- Microsoft Office

- Active listening

- Fully powered mechanical exoskeleton fused to my skin, tripling my physical endurance so I never have to take a break. I can also punch through concrete.

- No need for paternity leave, as I've opted to raise children like a gecko and abandon my babies at birth

- Never called in sick, even when I was physically disintegrating after being possessed by a small demon that would make me vomit so hard that my body would fly backward a hundred yards

Accolades

- Recipient of Nobel Prize in "Medicine and Finding a Customer's Lost Receipt"

- Awarded "Cleanest Break Room Microwave Post-Pasta Reheat" at my last job

- Once retweeted by the official Medieval Times account

Résumé Add-Ons

(These are some additions that are sure to make any résumé stand out.)

- Company-branded waterproof waist pouch containing forty dollars strapped to the front

- Personal shoulder massager (i.e., two mechanical arms attached to the top of the résumé that extend outward to massage the reader's shoulders)

- Perforated coupon at the bottom of the page for one free rotisserie chicken at the nearest Costco

- Eye of Karthon: The wicked eye of a nameless god lost to time with the power to hypnotize and command all who behold it.

JOB INTERVIEWS

Congrats! The employer loved your application, and you're off to the next overlong and torturous phase: the job interview. Sure, you've already answered all the relevant questions with the info on your résumé and cover letter, but they need to see how well you can lie about wanting the job *in person*.

In olden times, you could get a job by simply approaching a stranger and doing that medieval handshake where two people grab each other's forearms and shout "Well met!" But now, you must regale an interviewer with charming tales about efficiency, passion for teamwork, and that one time you went above and beyond by moving into your old boss's house and working as his butler for a month.

It's all about keeping the interviewer happy because, in this instance, they're the one who's always right. So you'll have to grit your teeth and smile as every question they ask reveals more and more red flags.

"Are you typically reachable in your off hours?"

"You're not planning to have kids, right?"

"How well do you handle incoming fire from a mortar cannon?"

The interviewer is sure to acknowledge your unflappability, once you nervously answer, "I actually thrive under fire from World War I artillery."

Of course, job interviews *should* be just as much about the company proving their worth to the employee, but it's hardly ever like that. In a perfect world, job interviews would be structured like *The*

Voice, where the candidate sits in a big red chair facing the other direction and doesn't hit the button to turn around until the company offers the right amount of money.

There are many types of job interviews: one-on-one, panels, over-the-phone, mid-haunted hayride. But the worst by far, in my opinion, is the acting audition. There's nothing more humiliating than pretending to be a British doula over Zoom for a casting director you thought was on mute, but in fact was just not laughing. Imagine you lose out on a job and discover the person who got it was Peter Dinklage. That *actually* happened to me once. My acting manager called me to let me know, and I was like, "Duh." I'm pretty sure I wouldn't have been invited to my sister's wedding if Peter Dinklage were available.

So how do you nail an interview? Simple. Tell charming stories, laugh at the interviewers' jokes, make them feel special, never let them see you sweat, keep the following thoughts in this chapter inside your head, and, most importantly, be Peter Dinklage.

JOB INTERVIEW RANTS

"Why do you want to work here?"

I don't. I'm sorry for the confusion. I thought my facial expression made that obvious. What I *want* is to sleep fourteen hours a day like a dog and spend the evenings dancing underneath a waterfall like no one's watching. But, sadly, I need money. That's why I'm here. I need cash, and I'm too shy to sell pictures of my feet online. Also, no one's asking for that. This might be a surprise, but my passion isn't chasing away dumpster divers trying to steal trash from T.J. Maxx. Do I want to work here? I don't even want to *be* here. *Will* I work here? Yes. Will I quit at the soonest opportunity? Also, yes.

"Are you comfortable working in a fast-paced environment?"

You mean "a poorly managed one"? A "fast-paced environment" is just corporate speak for "needlessly and unrelentingly stressful." Sounds like you need a bunch of self-starters with flexible schedules because whoever's in charge, in jargon terms, sucks asscheeks. But, sure, butter it up as "fast-paced." Glad to know I'm not the only one lying in this job interview. *Fast-paced*? Are we inside a MrBeast video for third graders? I'll be fast-paced for the first week, then I'll settle into my "I'm-no-longer-worried-about-being-fired-in-fact-I-welcome-it" pace. Trust me, the stakes aren't that high. We're processing returns, not defusing a nuke with three seconds to go.

"What's your greatest weakness?"

Not having rich parents. Or how about being unable to find a way to make money that didn't involve talking to you? I'm simply being honest. What do you want from me—a Jedi mind trick to make you think my weakness is my strength?

"Oh yes, my biggest fault is that I'm *too* productive."

"I'm addicted to that feeling of working a closing shift immediately followed by an opening shift, where I have to choose whether I'd rather sleep *or* eat."

"I'll drop whatever vial I'm holding in my hands to pick up a call from work, even if it's covered in a dozen biohazard warnings and I'm sure I'll hear a scientist whisper to himself, 'May God have mercy on us all,' as it hits the ground."

The truth is, my real weakness is I've shit my pants no less than three times as a grown adult. That's *way too many* times. That's enough times that there will likely be a fourth time, and if I'm working here forty hours a week, there's a good chance it's gonna be here.

"Where do you see yourself in five years?"

Interviewing for another job. And that job will probably be at least two jobs away from this one. I go through employers QUICK. I can already tell from this conversation that I won't be able to listen to you talk for more than five hours, let alone five years. Am I supposed to say I'm looking for an employer to finally settle down with? You should've scheduled this interview during cuffing season. That's a big commitment, buddy. Not even cults come on this fast. Why don't you buy me dinner first? I'm kidding, I want zero off-the-clock contact with you. And by dinner, I meant a bag of knock-off-brand Twizzlers from the break room vending machine called "Gene's Danglies" that I've never seen sold anywhere else. I understand you want to know I have goals. Well, here they are: within five years, a billionaire from Dubai will see one of my Instagram posts and invite me to live in his giant tower full of transparent glass floors that make me physically ill to walk on. If for some reason that doesn't happen and I'm still here, trust me, I won't be working. I'll be using company time to google "Where did I go wrong?"

"What are your greatest strengths?"

Lying in interviews. Remember thirty seconds ago when I said I'm a passionate self-starter? That couldn't be further from the truth. If I'm left alone in an Airbnb with a Roku full of streaming services the last guest forgot to log out of, you will never see me again. Also, I should let you know that I'm not the guy who did the high-wire walk between the Twin Towers in 1974, despite what it said on my résumé. That was a French man named Philippe Petit. And I didn't really miss breakfast. I brought in this box of baguettes just to keep up that previous charade. But why do you need anything more from me than showing up and doing the job? Everything else is just BS.

"I'm detail-oriented!"

"I'm creative!"

"I'm such a good team player that at my last position, the sheer force of my teamwork was enough to divert the path of an asteroid that was headed straight for Earth."

"I'm Philippe Petit!" (Sorry, I did it again.)

"We need to do a second interview."

Just tell me now! Were you not listening the first time? This is such a long, drawn-out process. Are you eliminating candidates one by one like *The Bachelor*? Are people watching this week-to-week? Let me guess, you got an order from CBS for eighteen episodes of me sitting in a room talking about what I think my greatest achievement is. End it here and now, I beg you. Or is this like *Survivor*, and every week I have to do a new challenge? "Last week you told us hypothetically what the title of your biography would be. Your challenge this week? Let's tie you to a post at high tide and see how long you can hold your breath underwater." Be careful, it's a slippery slope to *Squid Game*, my friends. How many levels to this game are there? Let's just cut to the chase. Make it a speedrun! Be honest, you don't even want to be doing this many interviews. Just give me the job, so this suffering will be over and the real suffering of working together can begin.

"How would you describe yourself in three words or less?"

Bad. At. Work.

"How would your coworkers describe you?"

Fun. To. Drink. With.

"Describe a time when you made a mistake."

vaguely gestures to the room

Do I even need to answer this one?

"Why did you leave your previous position?"

I walked in on a mob hit gone wrong in the back room, and Witness Protection assigned me to work here. Why do you think? It didn't pay enough. I didn't realize I needed an origin story to work at Planet Fitness. At my last job, I was being stalked by an evil doppelganger. A sick, twisted version of myself who also turned out to be a really great team player, so they replaced me with him. My values no longer align with my previous company's vision of trapping me in old-timey stocks and letting customers spit on me. I'm looking for a new challenge, and figuring out ways to pretend to work somewhere else seemed more fun than joining ISIS. The truth is I needed to work at a bigger building with more hiding spots because my old manager found all of mine.

"What would your former manager say about you?"

Pass.

"Tell me about a time when you worked on a team."

My old coworkers and I assembled ourselves into a human ladder to navigate our way through a giant hedge maze. We didn't want to be there, but the CEO at my last company got a hankering to hunt down the world's most dangerous prey: man. The rest is history. Come on, obviously I know how to work on a team. If employees weren't good team players, the entire world would be a smoldering pile of dust right now. The real answer is, at my last job, my team and I collectively decided every night *not* to perform an intricate heist where we robbed the store's vault after gracefully breakdancing our way past the laser security system. Despite having more than enough justification to do so.

"We'll be in touch."

Don't be. I know that one. I've been ghosted by jobs before. Is this because I spent forty-five minutes failing to do a back somersault after you asked about my special skills? It's your loss! Another forty-five and you would've seen magic!

"If you were a crayon, what color would you be?"

I'm an adult. And I don't want to talk about crayons because you forgot to read over your own job posting before you began this interview. What are you even saying right now? Is this really gonna help you determine if I'm qualified or not? How about instead of me explaining why I'd be fuchsia, you look at my résumé and see six years of customer service experience and give me the job based on that? You know, an actual *real* thing that matters? Why don't you ask a good question like, "Can you share an example of how you helped an escalated customer?" Or, "How is that planchette moving across the Ouija board on its own?!" See how easy it is to come up with these? Here's one more: *Why am I interviewing for this job when I should obviously have yours?* If we're just bringing up random things, why don't we skip the interview entirely, and I'll just hand you a DVD filled with videos of me diving into a pool? It'll be just as helpful in the hiring decision as discussing my favorite color. I mean, is there a wrong answer to the crayon question? How about red? And not because I'm a socialist. Because I'm pissed off.

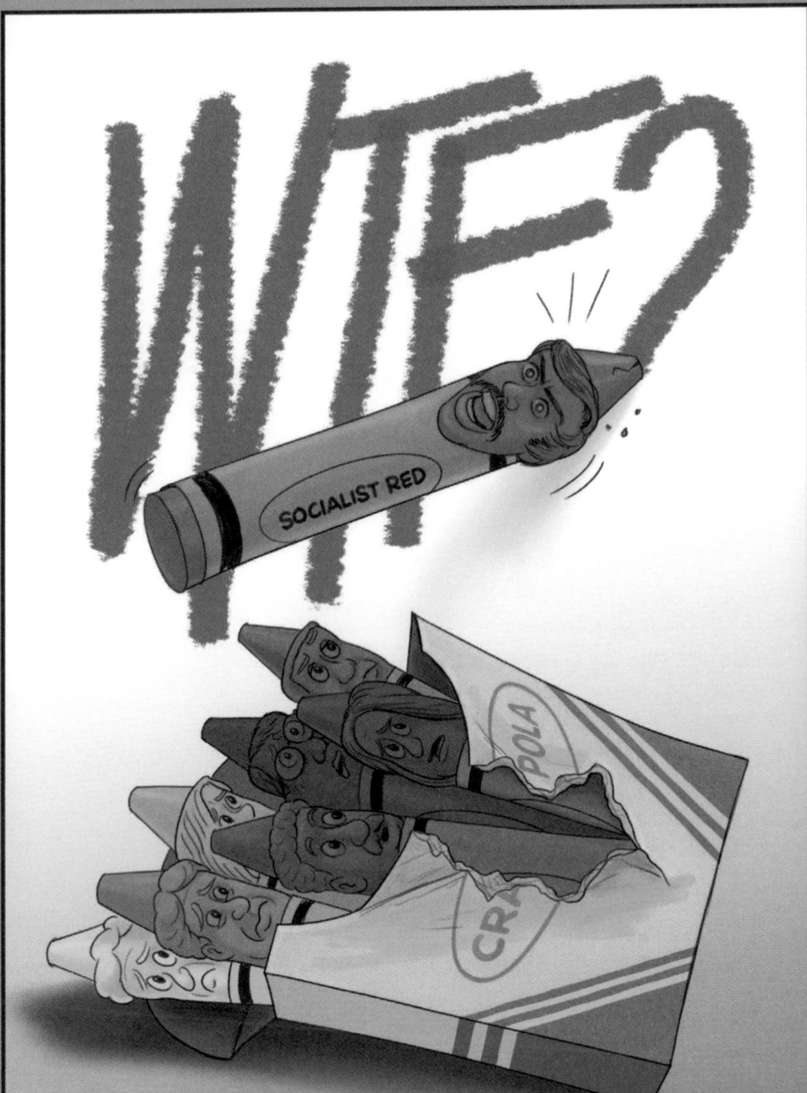
WTF?
SOCIALIST RED
CRA
POLA

REFERENCE FLOW CHART

When you need a reference to vouch for you, follow this flow chart to make sure you have the right person.

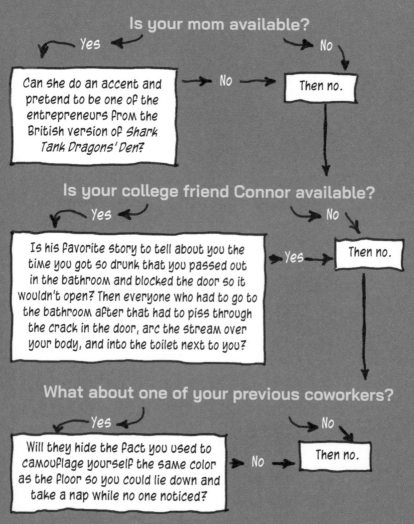

Is your mom available?

Yes ← ← → No

Can she do an accent and pretend to be one of the entrepreneurs from the British version of *Shark Tank Dragons' Den*? → No → Then no.

Is your college friend Connor available?

Yes ← → No

Is his favorite story to tell about you the time you got so drunk that you passed out in the bathroom and blocked the door so it wouldn't open? Then everyone who had to go to the bathroom after that had to piss through the crack in the door, arc the stream over your body, and into the toilet next to you? → Yes → Then no.

What about one of your previous coworkers?

Yes ← → No

Will they hide the fact you used to camouflage yourself the same color as the floor so you could lie down and take a nap while no one noticed? → No → Then no.

Should we even bother asking your previous manager?

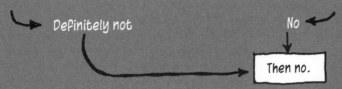

Definitely not

No

Then no.

Do you know Poseidon, god of the sea?

Yes

No

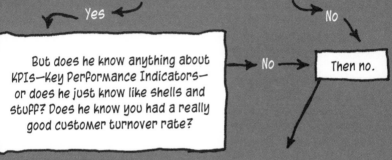

But does he know anything about KPIs—Key Performance Indicators— or does he just know like shells and stuff? Does he know you had a really good customer turnover rate?

No →

Then no.

Is your brother near you?

Yes

No

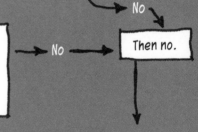

Can he stop talking about ChatGPT and how it's helping him finish his novel about a ghost who invents a phantom diaper to keep food from falling out of him?

No →

Then no.

Is there anyone else just sort of around outside?

Yes

Is it a street artist loudly playing the drums? And you're afraid to get close because it implies you're gonna give them some money?

→ Yes

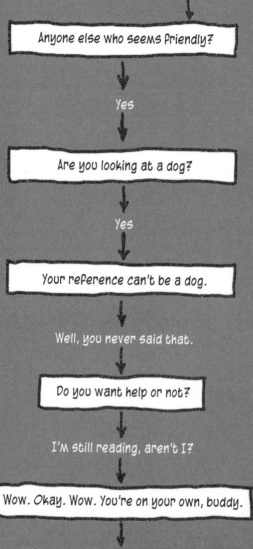

Anyone else who seems friendly?

Yes

Are you looking at a dog?

Yes

Your reference can't be a dog.

Well, you never said that.

Do you want help or not?

I'm still reading, aren't I?

Wow. Okay. Wow. You're on your own, buddy.

Come on. I'm sorry. I'm just frustrated and didn't get a lot of sleep last night. I was up all night rewatching that *MasterChef* season where Claudia won.

WHOA, WHOA, SPOILER ALERT! I was gonna watch that!

That season is almost ten years old! And she's got a bunch of cookbooks out that say "*MasterChef* winner."

Well, that's why I close my eyes and scream anytime I run through a bookstore.

Just don't go inside in the first place!

Yeah, yeah, if it was only that easy. . . . Is there any other human being walking by?

Yes

Do you have twenty bucks?

Yes

Then we've found our reference!

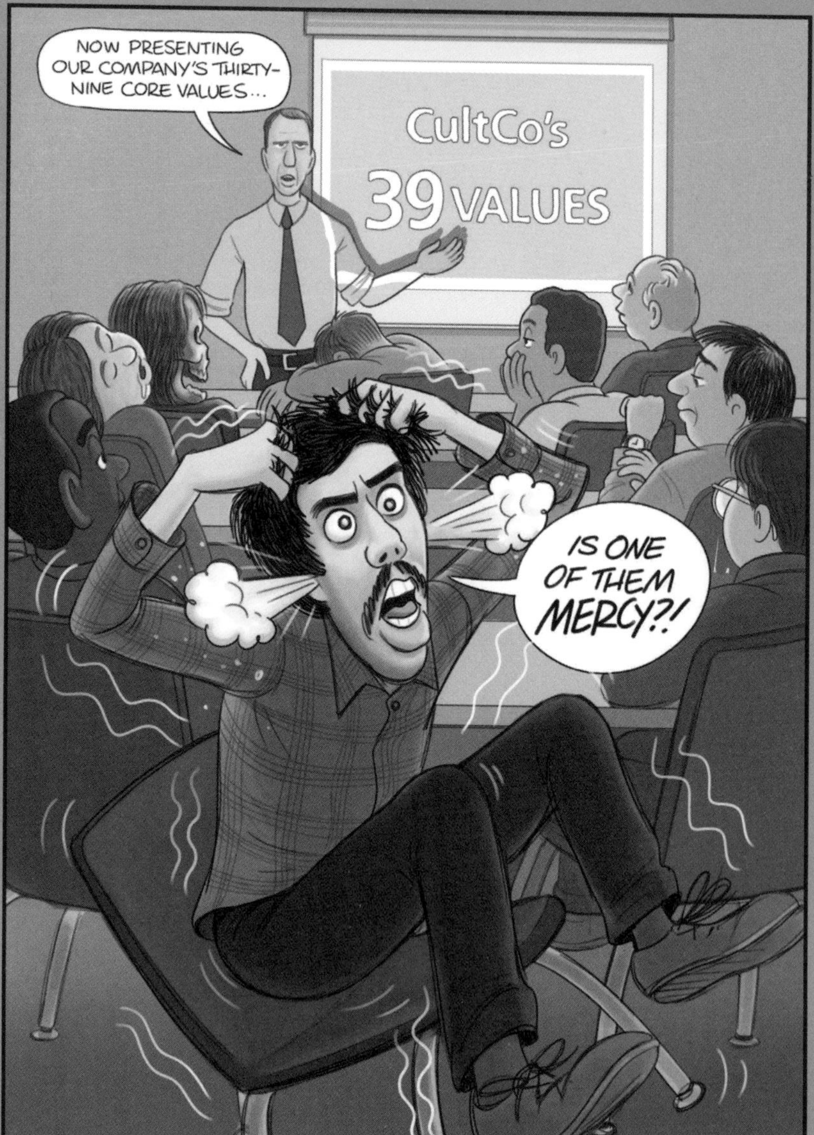
NOW PRESENTING OUR COMPANY'S THIRTY-NINE CORE VALUES...
CultCo's
39 VALUES
IS ONE OF THEM MERCY?!

CHAPTER 2

ORIENTATION

"Unfortunately, you got the job"

A fresh start. A new beginning. Your first day at the new job, and if you're anything like me, the last day you'll ever be on time again. It's a day full of excitement and wonder, and it normally begins with your manager stumbling out from behind a bunch of metal trashcans saying something like, "Oh shit, I forgot you started today. I don't even have you in the system yet." What system? How does it work? Literally no one here knows. But the system's the only thing that makes sure you get paid, and it has no idea who you are. So far, so good.

The first few shifts will consist of a process called *onboarding* (a word that my Baltimore accent refuses to let me pronounce properly). It includes meeting your new coworkers, filling out paperwork, and doing a lot of espionage work to deduce the minimum level of effort required to actually *do* the job and stay employed. You're basically an investigator, and your job is to figure out if the people here actually know what they're doing or if it's like any other workplace and they're all just pretending. During this phase, it's difficult not to sound like an extremely obvious undercover cop. "Boy, I sure do love work! I'm a regular old workaholic. But you know what I love even more than work? ILLEGAL CRIMES! KNOW OF ANY?"

Some jobs offer training during your first week, and others will simply abandon you in the woods like a Spartan baby forced to fend for itself. If you receive training, hopefully it'll be something a little more in-depth than the oldest employee looking at you with a haunted face while screaming, "Survive! That's the only advice I have, junior. Survive." But, of course, no matter the quality level, training for a job almost never resembles what the day-to-day work will actually entail. It's like someone googled "how to do this job" and then made a slideshow based off the fifteenth page of search results. Or a middle school boy who practices kissing on his bathroom mirror in case he ever dates someone who's a sentient piece of flat glass. You think you're prepared? You know nothing!

Companies are so obsessed with delivering monologues about their company culture and brand values, they often overlook the most crucial aspect of training: actually explaining how to do the f$#king job. They treat these little orientation seminars like Shakespeare—everyone has their own special take on them. "Oh wow! This company's cybersecurity presentation takes place in feudal Japan." "The safety demonstration was told exclusively via shadow puppets. I have no idea where the fire extinguisher is stored, but the performance was so moving."

Because you're so new, you slap on a fake smile and act like you're loving every minute of it. But here, you don't have to. Meeting new people, training, paperwork, employee handbooks, brand values— these are all terrible things I'm happy to make fun of. Also, keep in mind, your trainer probably doesn't want to be there either, so maybe you can start to build a friendship based on that.

TRAINING RANTS

"Are you sure you start today?"

Are you sure you should be in charge? I promise I wouldn't be here if I didn't. I double-checked and got here early because I'm still trying to make a good first impression. Apparently, you've given up on that. You think I'm coming in a week early for research? Yeah, this first visit is purely for academic purposes. And I've already learned you have no idea what you're doing. Do I start today? No, I'm here to tailgate my orientation. Figured I'd set up a grill in the parking lot a day or two beforehand and get a head start on the drinking problem this job will no doubt give me.

"I don't have anyone for you to shadow."

Great, I'll just guess how to do the job then. I'll put on a blindfold, spin around six times, and wander aimlessly toward the sound of customers breaking glass. Why would training be necessary? Just as baby sea turtles instinctively know to head toward the water after they hatch, humans are born with the innate knowledge of how to operate an ASSUR point-of-sale system. Are you a moron? I mean, seriously, what am I supposed to base my workday on? Dice rolls? Tea leaves? If something goes wrong, should I load a previous save? A complete lack of training makes talking with customers even worse than it already is. It's like a trivia game where no one knows the answers.

"Was Millard Fillmore the thirteenth president of the United States?"

I don't know, was he?

Well, the back of the card doesn't have an answer. It just says, *"Good luck, idiots."*

But, hey, maybe it's better this way. Whoever I shadowed would probably end up resenting me because I'd be forcing them to relearn how to do the job by the book just to teach me . . . so I can immediately unlearn it. And don't think I didn't clock the fact that *you* can't train me, because we both know you don't know how to do anything here besides *not* schedule people for training.

"Welcome to the madhouse! Prepare yourself. We got a lot of characters working here."

I need you to settle down. *Characters*? You mean two women named Jeanne? Somebody bust out the straitjackets. Apparently these two really need their coffee in the morning. How has no one based a cinematic universe around you people? We don't need characters at work. We need people to chill out. I know everyone wants to be special, but some people at work try way too hard to have a "thing." So instead of loudly shouting, "I'm crab walk guy!" before dropping to all fours and scurrying into the back room, maybe we can just talk about what podcasts we like and relax.

"Make sure to read the employee handbook cover to cover."

To save money on Ambien? Great idea. No offense, but I don't read anything unless there's a dead body and an alcoholic detective by page five. I'll do you a great honor and pretend to read it. Now your handbook joins the likes of *Watership Down*, *The Great Gatsby*, and most texts in my family group chat. Honestly, I could probably guess everything that's in here. I'll take a wild swing and say your code of conduct includes respect and professionalism. Thank goodness I read that, I was *this* close to tearing off my shirt, covering myself in vaseline, and seeing how far I could slide across the floor. I didn't realize this place had rules, otherwise I would've immediately turned the stock room into an illegal gambling ring/underground vermin fight club.

"Here, we think 'customer first.'"

And employee last. That's why you've got a "Now Hiring" sign in your window so old, you can see the words "No Irish Need Apply" crossed out at the bottom. Hate to break it to you, but this isn't really a fresh take. "Oh wow, a business that prioritizes how they make money. How refreshing." You want to be original? Open up training by saying, "Here, we think downhill mountain biking first. So everyone grab a Go-Pro, and hold the hell on." Companies love to say they're "customer first" and then proceed to make those customers just as miserable as the people who work there.

"At this store, we're a family."

No, we're coworkers. What do you think this is? *Fast & Furious 10* . . . dollars an hour? Hate to break it to you, but I've applied to forty other "families" this week. We're not family; we're acquaintances who keep our lunch in the same fridge. This is just a job. Admit it, you're only calling us a family because you're gonna force us to spend Thanksgiving night together.

"This company was founded in 1968 by a young man with nothing more than a dream."

Are you ramping up to a musical number? He famously said, "I'm getting out of this town, I tell ya. I'm gonna be somebody. You hear that, Ma? Your boy's gonna be somebody . . . *2, 3, 4!*" Do I need the whole history? Is this some sort of dystopian indoctrination? I know you're trying to communicate the culture here, but it really sounds like some device is about to pry open my eyelids so you can show me a propaganda PowerPoint. A full slideshow of your founder wearing a series of nicer and nicer leather jackets until I believe he's the coolest person on Earth. We're one step away from you telling me the store has its own daily Pledge of Allegiance where we swapped the word "God" to "the people who made Little Caesars."

"Now presenting our company's thirty-nine core values."

Is one of them "mercy"? I'm tapping out. I'm calling uncle. I can't listen to someone rephrase the word *teamwork* thirty-nine times in a row. Did someone get a thesaurus for their birthday or something? I know whoever wrote this handbook was very proud of themselves for googling synonyms for *integrity*, but how about you whittle it down to three and let us get back to our lives? Good lord, thirty-nine values, and not a single one says "living wage." And how are they all "core"? No one has a *core* group of thirty-nine friends. That's called an army. Your company has more values than the study of mathematics. Edit yourself! And this is coming from a guy who wrote an entire book just to say "work sucks."

"Our brand values are teamwork, accountability, and communication."

Until your shift starts. Then, our values are stress, chaos, and your manager inviting themselves to happy hour.

"Our company's mission is to empower everyday people for a prosperous future."

I'm pretty sure that's exactly what the bad guy from *The Incredibles* wanted. Why does every company mission statement sound like an ominous threat from a villain who just kidnapped the mayor with a big butterfly net? "Be the leader that helps everyone find their happy place." Is that a line from the Joker's first comic book appearance? Nope, it's inexplicably the vision statement for JOANN Fabric and Crafts.

"Let's role-play through a few hypothetical work scenarios."

Well, we're already nailing the bad training scene. First of all, it should be illegal to say *role-play* at work. And are we really so desperate that we've resorted to doing improv with each other? The first rule of improv is supposed to be "yes, and," but when it's improv at work, that rule swaps to a "No! Please God, no!" Before we start, I need to know if this scenario takes place in an alternate universe where I'm paid enough to take this seriously. Also, these walkthroughs are always so tame. I don't need to train for how to help a reasonable customer return an item. I need training for the wild stuff! What about when a couple comes in demanding the store pay their legal fees after selling them a table with an assembly process so complex, it became "the straw that broke the divorce camel's back"? How about when a mother claims we knowingly sold her a crib that was haunted by the ghost of an old naval captain who's covered in rotting barnacles and is really bad with children? What then? Give me the training scenario for *that*!

"To sign up for health insurance, simply read through all fourteen orientation packets and fill out nine hundred pounds of onboarding forms."
Please just let me live. The amount of plans and information in here is literally incomprehensible. I just want to go to the doctor and easily obtain an antidote whenever I accidentally ingest a bubbling vial of bright green poison with vapors that turn into a skull upon opening. Is that so much to ask? I don't even care that the plans are so needlessly complicated, they're obviously ripping me off somehow. Why do so many employers control our access to health care? Why does health insurance never cover the care we actually require? I'm too tired from work to figure it out, so just sign me up, I guess.

"Early is on time, and on time is late."

That's not how words work. "Early is on time. Dogs are elevators. And imbecile is *you*." What are you even talking about? Somebody must have mixed up their flashcards when they were studying vocab last night. Words don't just mean anything you want. We live in a world with dictionaries and rules, and one of those rules is if I'm here at nine a.m., you have to shut up. You love to worry about when I start work, but you don't give a damn about making sure I leave on time. If I start early, then I'm leaving early. In a perfect world, I'd cram myself into one of those air-powered pneumatic tubes that old-timey office buildings use for mail, and it would blast me right to work in less than a second. That way I'd never be here for longer than I have to be. But until I can do that without shattering every bone in my body, I'll be waiting in my car until my shift's exact start time—and no sooner.

"You'll get your schedule for next week on Saturday night."

That's basically next week! Why do you insist on delivering my schedule every week via flash-bang? Trust me, I'm not worried about spoilers. Tell me in advance. Are you planning a surprise party? Just skip the confetti cannons, and let me know what day I can go grocery shopping next week, so I can buy food to live and continue doing this job. I don't want to wait for a schedule to go up like I'm a theater kid anxiously awaiting the cast list for the school play. "Yay! I got the part of 'sad man working Friday night and woefully staring out storefront window.' My dream role!"

"You're working a clopen this week. A closing shift, immediately followed by an opening shift."

I guess I'll sleep when I'm dead. No, no, no, it makes perfect sense to leave work and then start again five hours later. We all know scientists recommend sleeping for only ninety minutes each night. And people have the nerve to come up to me the next day and ask, "Where's your energy?" Or, "Why do you look so tired?" Because I *am*! I'm spending so little time in bed, my sleep paralysis demon is starting to worry. He filed a police report last night for a missing person. He's sweet like that. But who cares about my sleep schedule? I had to be here at six a.m. to make sure the store was open so those four old women had something to walk past while they did their morning laps.

"You need to change your work password every fourteen days."

How about every fourteen seconds, just to be safe? Are we holding account numbers for our rewards program or a list of every foreign diplomats' allergies? We don't need this much security. While we're at it, add a couple multi-million-dollar retinal scanners to the microwave in the break room, so no one can steal my Lean Cuisine. I don't even update my bank password. If PetSmart gets hacked and the first and last names of every person who bought one of those weird tongue-shaped cat brushes you hold in your mouth gets leaked, then so be it. They made their bed. I'm kidding, I'll change it. But get ready for the same word followed by a 1, then a 2, then a 3, and so on until I quit or die.

"What days are you available to work?"

Why give me false hope? You know what days you need me here, so make the schedule and let this charade end. But if you want the real answer, it's not in days. I was hoping I'd give you a series of forty-five-minute windows every week, and you could pick from one or two of those at most.

"Do you anticipate missing work for personal reasons?"

Constantly. In fact, one of my biggest reasons is that I personally don't like this place.

"At this company, we have a culture of freedom, not control."

Then allow me to change my pay to $75,000 a day. I'm simply expressing myself and exercising my freedom. Also, what's the code for the vault downstairs? Does DICK'S Sporting Goods even *have* a vault? No worries, if not. I see some gear I could use.

"Please remember this handbook is not 100 percent comprehensive."

Then what's the point of it?! This sounds like something hurriedly said at the end of a pharmaceutical ad for a drug that cures your overactive bladder at the cost of growing a second head that's visibly way more attractive than you. The hand-wringing does not inspire confidence. Remember how comforting it was when the flight attendant ended their safety presentation by announcing, "Please keep in mind that information wasn't intended to be 100 percent comprehensive. There are several crucial details we purposefully left out." Then you noticed the oxygen mask had a bike lock around it and your life vest was inside of a handcrafted puzzle box. No? Well, it wasn't as comforting as it sounds. Did you say "this isn't 100 percent comprehensive" just to keep the company out of legal trouble? If I get attacked by a mountain lion while on the clock, does that mean you can say, "Well, we told you the handbook wasn't comprehensive, so you really should've prepared for that." Then don't even write a handbook, just hand me a piece of paper that says, "Anything can and will happen. The universe is one big, chaotic pinball machine set to 'multi-ball,' and we're all trapped inside. Welcome to the Macy's team."

TYPES OF QUESTIONS SEEN ON EMPLOYEE TRAINING QUIZZES

The ones from a company that's been hurt before

1. Upon leaving your position, will you provide the appropriate amount of notice to your manager? Or will you simply walk out . . . just like Steven did?

    a. I will give the appropriate amount of notice.

    b. I'm just as bad as Steven.

2. Do you know Steven? If so, does he ever mention us?

    a. I don't know Steven.

    b. I do. He misses you.

The one you'll pass unless you really love confessing to crimes

You come across a big pile of cash in the back room with a sticky note that says, "This money is for your boss's critical brain surgery scheduled to start in thirty minutes." What do you do?

   a. Rob your boss blind with a big grin on your face, not a care in the world for his brain.

   b. Don't rob your boss.

The one that literally treats you like a child

What sound does a cow make?

- a. Moo.

- b. I don't see what this has to do with the job. Also, I don't know.

The one that definitely seems like a trick

Jigsaw, the full-on murderer from the horror franchise *Saw*, rolls up to the store trying to buy supplies for his next game. Do you ring him up? Keep in mind, in this scenario, you have no knowledge of his crimes. But you're getting bad vibes *for real*. But also, like, what are you gonna do? You're not a cop. Your job is to ring him up. But, again, it's Jigsaw, you know? Also, a rooster lays an egg on top of the store. Which way does it roll?

- a. Help Jigsaw as though he's any customer. And roosters don't lay eggs.

- b. Do not help Jigsaw. And the rooster's egg rolls to the east.

The one that's testing your loyalties

3. A coworker comes in, dressed in one of those sick wing-suits extreme sport athletes use to glide like flying squirrels. It's clear he's planning to go base jumping any second now and hasn't told your manager yet. What do you do?

   a. Throw on a wingsuit of your own, and perform a secret handshake with your coworker before skipping out.

   b. Tell your manager, even though that's incredibly lame.

The one that's deeply assessing your ability to work as a team player through an incredibly complex line of query

A coworker asks for help ringing up a customer. What's your first instinct?

   a. Help them.

   b. Trap them in a genie's lamp and bury them in sand for a hundred years.

The safety question that makes you wonder if this place is way more dangerous than you thought

As often happens, a vat of liquid mercury spills onto the workplace floor and a giant industrial fan activates, blowing all the mercury directly toward your face. What would be the recommended safety procedure?

    a.   Scream "AHHH! That's a lot of mercury!"

    b.   Turn on another industrial fan near you, keeping the mercury suspended in midair between the dueling fans until poison control can arrive.

The one cybersecurity question that makes you wonder if anyone at this job has ever used a computer before

You receive an email from JimmyTheDude@TheMafia.com asking to share your work password. How do you respond?

    a.   Shatter the screen with a hammer to prevent a data leak.

    b.   Turn the computer in to the FBI.

The one from a company that's clearly been the employer of Wile E. Coyote and wants to ensure they never make that mistake again

A customer claims one of their recently purchased items was damaged. What are your next steps?

a. Apologize for the inconvenience and order a replacement item.

b. Process a refund for the item and offer a coupon as compensation.

c. Strap yourself to a giant ACME rocket and fire it straight into the side of a canyon, flattening your body a half-second before your doomed vessel explodes.

Excerpts from an Employee Handbook That Hasn't Been Updated in 900 Years

Hidden deep in the forbidden section of an ancient library, covered in nearly a millennium's worth of dust, is an employee handbook that your boss outright refuses to update. Like most handbooks, the information contained within is horrifically outdated and irrelevant. But it's all you've got to go on, so good luck.

☞ "Adherence to dress code includes a ripped tunic covered in mud and fleas, armor plates sporting the company logo, and permitted flair."

☞ "To help a customer recover a lost receipt, please consult the water witch who lives in the town's well. Simply toss down one of the customer's eyelashes along with their youngest child, and the witch will gain knowledge of the customer's entire past, present, and future—including the date they bought that end table."

☞ "Discounts can be offered to customers willing to barter with a pair of oxen or a large dairy cow, so long as the animals have been blessed by the local master of the hunt or royal guardian of the forest."

☞ "Build rapport with a customer by bonding over shared knowledge that the sun revolves around the Earth and that the nobles of the kingdom have the ability to control the weather."

- "If counting systems are down for longer than thirty minutes, initiate a hard reboot by sacrificing the eldest goat in the village on the shop doorstep and shouting for the gods to witness you."

- "Payment will be distributed on a biweekly basis in the form of a stack of cheese wheels to be feasted upon by the employee's family."

- "If you become ill with a mild case of the common cold and haven't been cured by a simple blood draining, please clock out and find a quiet place to die. There's no saving you. You've more than likely been cursed by a forest troll and doomed to turn to ash. You will be missed."

- "The only tolerable excuse for tardiness is if you were run down in the street by the baron's carriage pulled by thirty-five wild boars. You must exhibit hoof marks on your back, or you will be written up."

- "At this shop, we adhere to the general rule of two-week notice by combat. For your leave to be accepted, you will be required to fire your resignation letter into your manager's chest via crossbow or defeat them in a one-on-one swordfight."

- "You get a thirty-minute unpaid lunch break."

A FIELD GUIDE TO THE COWORKERS YOU'LL MEET AT EVERY JOB

Coworkers. A rare bright spot in one of my least favorite parts of existence: other people. Your fellow workers get you. You get them. They're the only other people on Earth who understand your work language. If you say, "Run me a scrub report through the ILX system and leave a copy of the 'blurgnon' printout on my desk," most people would reply, "Sorry, what? Were those real words, or were you ordering appetizers at a space cantina?" But not your coworkers. They'd know. In some ways, they know more about you and your life than anyone else, but they're also the people you'll immediately cut ties with after you find a job that offers health insurance so good you can finally afford to remove the human tail you were born with.

When you start a new job, you'll want to build relationships with your coworkers ASAP. It's like you're on a season of *Big Brother* that will last the next forty-five years of your life. As you go, you'll find a core group of work besties, a few work acquaintances, and, inexplicably, one work archnemesis you hate with every fiber of your being. Why? Maybe it's because you overslept and came in late one time, and every day since they've referred to you as "Mayor Snooze" and it pisses you off to no end. Eventually, on your last day, you two will battle each other on top of a waterfall while the rest of the staff surrounds you chanting ancient war cries. But for now, this is the getting-to-know-you phase. Consult the field guide in the following pages to identify these all-too-common types of coworkers.

The Hustler

- Claims to love "the grind" but doesn't do any work at the job that actually pays them money

- Lists "entrepreneur" in all of their social media bios, even though they don't own a single business

- Rooted for the wrong people in *Parasite*

- Will join any pyramid scheme as long as it's run by a guy yelling, "Here's how I make $15,000 a week by simply owning a laptop"

- Refers to themselves as a "digital growth sherpa" because the local weatherman reacted to their Instagram Story once

The One Who Is Living for Drama

- Always dropping ominous details, hoping someone will ask a follow-up question about their life:

  "I might not be in tomorrow . . . because of the test results."

  waits to see if anyone takes the bait

  "Most people can say they've never been the target of an assassination attempt, but not me . . . not anymore."

  stares wildly at the room, desperately hoping someone finds them interesting

- Their emails contain at least seven different fonts

- First to tell everyone at work when a celebrity dies

The Mystery

- Never mentions a single detail of their personal life, to the point where everyone genuinely believes they went through the *Severance* procedure

- Stops mid-conversation with a customer when their shift ends and whispers, "My time here is done," before disappearing in a cloud of smoke

The Clinger

- Constantly suggests the whole team get together after work, creating the most dead air you've ever experienced in a break room

- Recommends fifteen podcasts to you every single day

- Somehow remembers every detail about everything you've ever told them; you, however, just realized you've been calling them "Pean" instead of their actual name "Dean" for about six months straight

The Parent Whose Stories About Their Kids Ensure You Will Never Want to Have Any

- Appears to have never slept, like, ever. Not even once.

- Loves to explain that many eleven-year-olds still haven't grown out of the biting phase

- Constantly on the phone with their child's principal, and from what you can tell, the kid seems to be a Jimmy Neutron–level domestic terrorist

The Weirdos Who Use the Terms "Work Wife" and "Work Husband"

- They're quiet-quitting their actual marriages

The Futurist

- Always looking for the next gig

- Never stops applying for other jobs. You've even caught them googling "How to become an air traffic controller" and "Fake air traffic controller certification (printable)."

- Dreams of buying farmland and becoming self-sustaining, despite possessing none of the skills to do so

- Loosens screws on shelves in hopes said shelves will topple over and crush them, leading to a big lawsuit payout and a life in a seemingly ideal state: comatose but rich

The Flake

- Always calling off from work

- Whenever they *are* present, there's a pretty good chance it's just a life-size cardboard cutout of them, or a mannequin in a wig with a picture of their face stapled to the head

- Exclusively volunteers to bring the plates and cups to the work potlucks—aka "the coward's choice"

The Person Who Showers at Work

- Bro. Like, *what*? I didn't think those showers worked. Someone's actually using them? Really feels like they're using this as a loophole just to be naked at work. Not a fan.

The Ghost of Christmas Past

- Turns out working one-third of one day of the year doesn't pay the bills, so even *they* had to pick up a second job

- Really good at remembering everyone's drunken mistakes at every holiday party ever

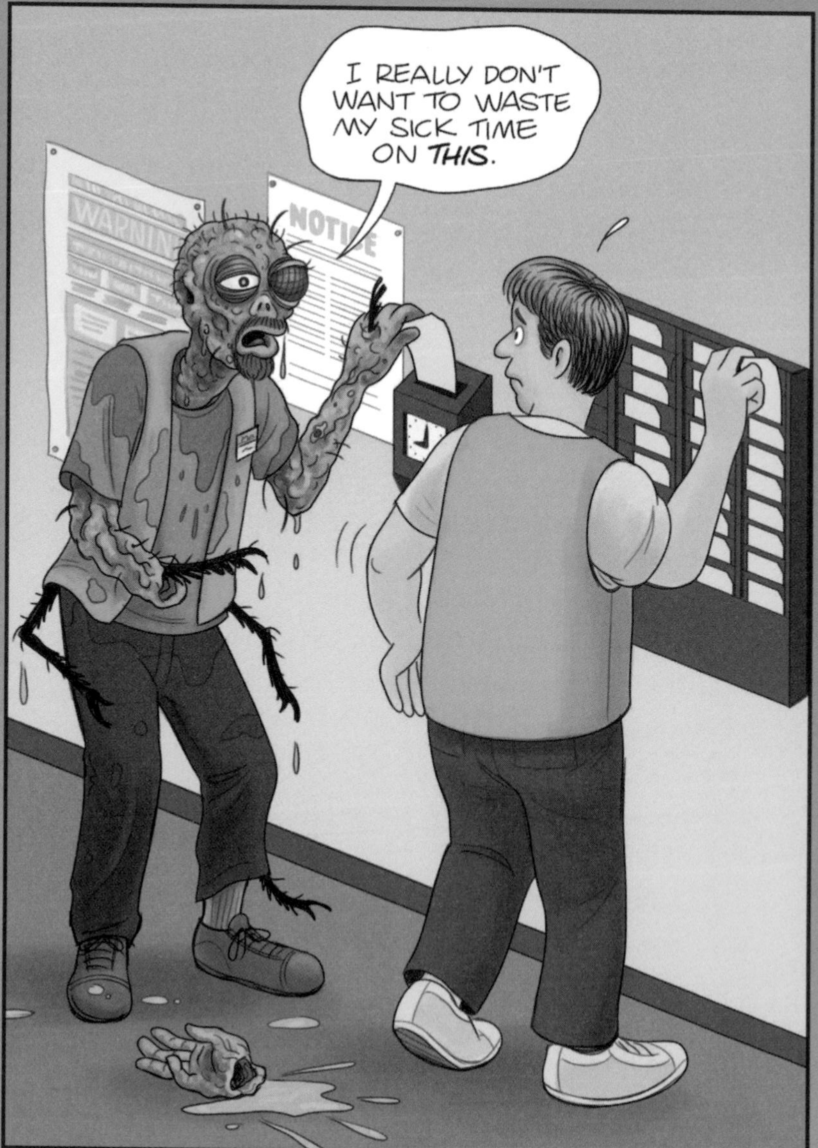
I REALLY DON'T WANT TO WASTE MY SICK TIME ON *THIS*.

The Guy Who Is Actively Transforming into a Fly

Clearly they activated a teleportation chamber at the exact moment a fly flew in, and now they've been turned into a hideous monstrosity. But they have a limited number of sick days, and they're already planning on using what they have to go see Taylor Swift in New Orleans next month. So they decided to still come to work today. It's admirable and disgusting.

Kevin Hart

What the hell? That's literally Kevin Hart? Wow, that man really is a workaholic. He got a job here, and he's using his break to film another Draft Kings commercial.

The Make-A-Wish Kid Who Definitely Overestimated How Cool It Would Be to Work at the Mall

"Um, can I get a redo on that wish? I'll take a day in the NBA instead."

The Person Who Brings in Donuts

Everyone loves this person. Be this person. I would die for this person.

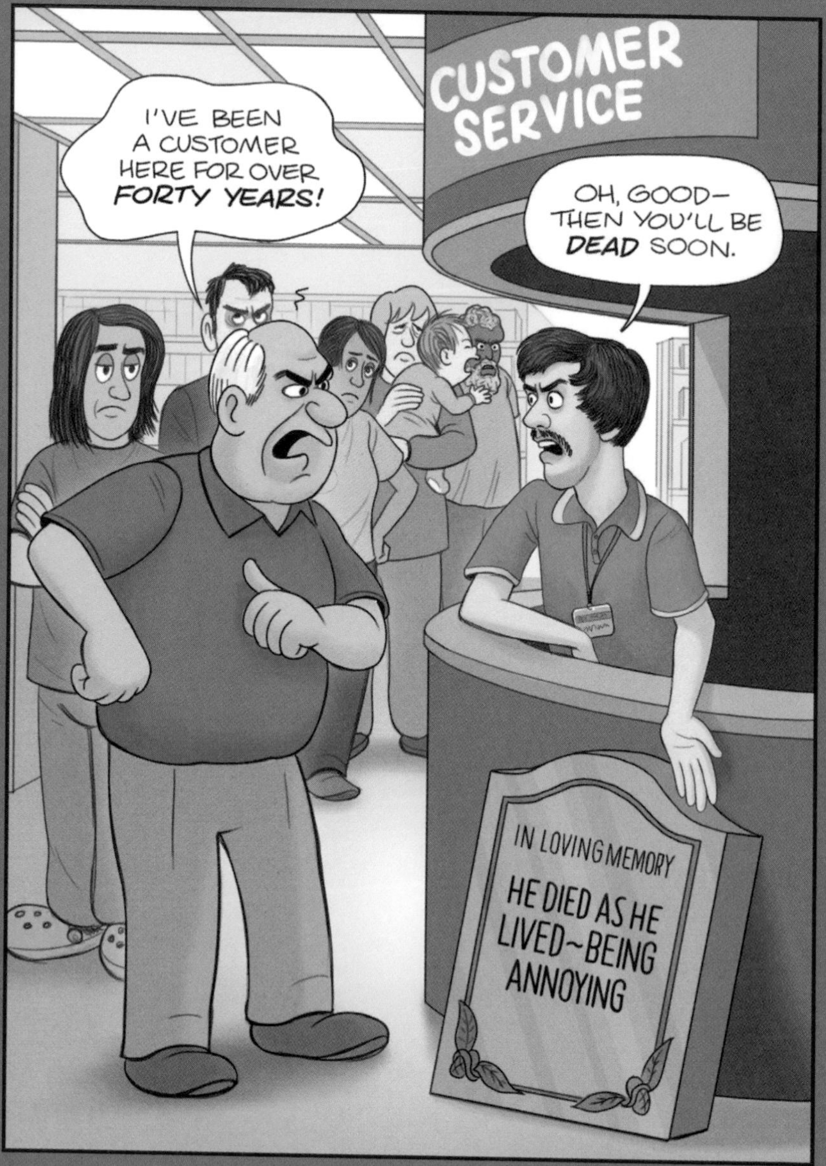
CUSTOMER SERVICE
I'VE BEEN A CUSTOMER HERE FOR OVER FORTY YEARS!
OH, GOOD— THEN YOU'LL BE DEAD SOON.
IN LOVING MEMORY
HE DIED AS HE LIVED~BEING ANNOYING

CHAPTER 3

CUSTOMER SERVICE

"The customer is always wrong"

You know that thing when you're changing a baby's diaper, and then all of a sudden, the baby just starts pissing on you? That pretty much sums up what it feels like to work in customer service. You're looking at this baby like, "Dude, why would you do this to me? I'm literally the only person in this room trying to help you right now, and you're actively urinating on me. And giggling about it." That's customer service.

And you never know what's going to happen. Sometimes customers are nice, sometimes they're not. Every interaction is a game of Russian roulette with your mental health. Will the next person coming your way be a reasonable human being or the star of YouTube's "Epic Customer Freakout Compilation #9"?

Working in customer service is like opening one of those little Advent calendars. You pop open one day, and there's a little piece of chocolate inside. You pop open another, and there's a fifty-year-old adult man trying to spit on you because he misread a coupon. It's an exhausting, thankless job. But if it's any consolation, at least the pay is horrible and there's little to no benefits. Hats off to anyone who's ever done it.

Generally, people assume customer service workers are lazy, joyless brick walls of unhelpfulness. That's insane. They're passionate, hardworking employees with a sense of humor that only comes from seeing the absolute worst of humanity.

At my stand-up shows, I've heard people tell stories about customers asking employees to babysit their father's ashes while they shopped, inviting the staff to weirdo mask-required sex parties, selling cocaine in the frozen food aisle and filing a complaint when asked to leave—and, of course, the complaint I hear most frequently without fail: customers just straight-up taking a dump on the floor. That's literally 90 percent of the messages I receive. I even met a department store security guard in Rochester, New York, who told me one day a customer sauntered over to the clearance section and just emptied their bowels in one of the purses.

On the rack.

In broad daylight.

Suffice to say, customer service employees are dealing with way more than they should ever have to, and they still get the job done.

If customer service workers get a bad reputation, it's because they're rarely empowered by their companies to provide timely and effective solutions. Most companies send them out into the world like rodeo clowns meant to distract a bull. These employees are human stress balls meant to be poked and squeezed. They're the raw chicken dangling from Steve-O's jockstrap as he shimmies across a tightrope above a pit of alligators in a *Jackass* stunt, the sacrificial meat designed to take all the damage so the company, represented here by Steve-O's nether regions, can make it across unscathed. Obviously, this kind of work takes a toll on you.

It's a vicious cycle. Customer service workers are made to feel powerless by the companies they work for, and then they're thought of as idiots by the customers they're supposed to help. I know from experience. During my time at a call center, I heard every customer issue a thousand times over, and my team continuously tried to get the company to address the structural issues that led to these kinds of complaints.

But they never did.

"Who cares if our customers are unhappy because their merchandise arrived damaged after we delivered it via a blunderbuss shot at their house? We're still making money!"

It might surprise some people, but I was actually very good at customer service, even outside of the call center. I worked for several years as an actor for a murder mystery dinner theater, where I had to constantly solve customer issues while pretending I was a speakeasy owner in 1923.

Customer: "There's something wrong with my food!"

Me, in an insane mid-Atlantic accent: "Oh, no! Has it been *poisoned*?"

Customer: "No, it's cold."

Me, dropping the act immediately: "Oh, my God, I'm so sorry about that."

It was ridiculous, and fun as hell. Among all my jobs, I saw the full range of customers out there. Why are there so many bad ones? My theory is people feel so powerless in the world and stressed out economically that when they get a chance to be dominant over someone else—like a cashier—they abuse it.

Of course, most customer interactions you'll have at work will be perfectly fine, sometimes even good. Every once in a while, you'll meet a customer who is so nice, they completely restore your faith in humanity, and you start hearing Whoville music in your head while your little Grinch heart grows three times in size. But this chapter isn't about *those* customers. It's about the worst ones.

CUSTOMER SERVICE RANTS

"You just lost yourself a customer."

Do you think I own this business? I'm not an undercover boss. This mustache is real. I'm not in disguise. I *chose* to look like if Ted Lasso did meth. "You just lost a customer." Oh, no. I guess I'll just continue making minimum wage. Like what? I don't care about the company's profit margin. If this place goes out of business, I'm off tomorrow. Do you expect me to get on the phone with headquarters? "Hey, Sweden, we're about to lose Cathy in White Marsh, Maryland. You don't seem to understand how important this is. We stand to lose fifteen dollars if she walks. This could sink us. She tried to buy something on sale, but it was just *next* to the thing that was *actually* on sale. There were nine signs, but she maintains it's still our fault." Please. See you when you're back here next week.

"Can you just check in the back?"

Can you just accept *WE DON'T HAVE IT*? The back ain't some magical place. What do you think is back there, Santa's workshop? A portal to another universe where the only difference is that this store has a slightly larger stock room? The only thing back there is a clipboard with our schedules and some brownies Darcy brought in. You think the back is where I go to hide merchandise? The back is where I go to *cry*. If I had the stuff, I'd give it to you. Trust me when I say that you no longer being here is my biggest priority right now.

"I've been a customer here for over forty years."

Oh, good, then you'll be dead soon. I'll turn off the fluorescents so you can tell which light you're supposed to head toward. Are you trying to get a discount or a spot in our In Memoriam reel? Don't worry, I'll clap when your picture comes up. Sorry to tell you, but there's no lifetime achievement award for spending four decades putting things back on the wrong shelf at Big Lots. Are you wondering what kind of retirement plans we offer customers? Whatever it is, it's probably better than mine.

"I'm telling all my friends not to shop here."

Tell them. You think I want five other yous running around the store? I hope you realize you're threatening me with something positive. It's like you're a mugger approaching me from behind at an ATM, but instead of pressing a gun into my back, you're using a fifty-dollar gift card to Outback Steakhouse. How about this: have your friends call me, and I'll tell them myself. You think you hate this place more than me? I *work* here!

"I know the sale ended last week, but can I still get a discount?"

Do you hear yourself? We can't go backward. Time marches on. You want the sale from fifteen years ago too? When does it end, Diane? Most people go back in time to stop dictatorships. You're trying to get a two-for-one candle deal. You want that price? You're gonna have to go through the quantum realm with Ant-Man.

"Do you know how much I spend here?"

It doesn't matter! We don't thank our donors. This isn't PBS. Save your money. And my time. Shop somewhere else.

"I'd like to speak to your manager."

I'd like to speak to your mother. Tell her she should be embarrassed. She raised someone to act like a baby in public. I'm kidding, that's not fair. Only you deserve the credit for how much of an idiot you are. You want to speak to the manager? You think because they carry a few extra keys on their lanyard, they have the power to move mountains? The manager doesn't know what's going on. Haven't you ever worked anywhere before?

"The website said it was in stock."

What do your eyes say? Sometimes the website is wrong. It also has pictures of employees smiling. You see that here? There's a lot of misinformation online. I can post an AI-generated image of me marrying Magneto, but my lawyers still won't allow me to list his name anywhere in my estate planning. Go home and yell at your computer instead of me. It'll get you the same result: nothing.

"This is cheaper at other stores."

Then shop there. Why are you here? Do you need directions? You want me to call you an Uber? I don't control the prices. I'm a seasonal employee. What am I even supposed to say to that? "Oh, other stores offer this for cheaper, huh? I'll be sure to bring that up at the next town hall meeting where we all vote on how much to charge."

"You should open up more registers."

And who's gonna work them? You think I'm the only one up here because I called dibs? Go ahead and apply. You clearly see we're short-handed. Where's your résumé?

"The customer is always right."

About what? How to piss me off? You think you're God because you went shopping? You're not infallible; you're at the mall. The customer is always right, huh? That's why you're on your ninth try hitting the button for credit.

"Do you have any coupons for me?"

That's what I ask *you*. What? You think you just found a cheat code for the store? Oh yeah, I keep a few 100-percent-offs back here for the smart customers. Bring your own.

"It didn't scan. It must be free."

And you must be out of your mind to think you're the first person to say that to me. You're not even the first one today. Don't worry about the scan. I'll type in the product code and charge you double. I swear, I fake laugh at this job so much, I forgot how my real one sounds.

"You're open for ten more minutes? I'll be quick."

Quickly moving to the exit? This ain't a basketball game; we're not playing to the buzzer. You had the option to either hold a bunch of minimum wage workers hostage or go shopping tomorrow. You chose wrong. Get out.

"Do you work here?"

Obviously, yes. How many people do you know who wear a nametag recreationally? You think I'm behind the counter because I got lost? Do I work here? No, I'm dressed like this because I'm going to the midnight premiere of *IKEA: The Movie*.

"I'm just looking!"

And I'm just saying hi. I'm not trying to sell you something. I'm trying to have one interaction at work that makes me feel like a human being. I have feelings too. I'm a Pisces.

"You should smile more."

I'm a cashier, not a Rockette. I had to come to work today. There's no rule that said I had to enjoy it. You want me to smile? Well, we don't always get what we want. Why do you think I'm here?

"I'm returning this, but I don't have the receipt."

Then you're not returning it. I don't have the patience to explain that's exactly what you need a receipt for. Is this your first time in a store?

"You look bored. Let me give you something to do."

Nope. Start again. That was so wrong, you should have the big red X from *Family Feud* over your face. *Let* you give me something to do? I didn't even want to *let* you in the store. Of course I'm bored. It's called being at work.

"You must love working customer service. You get to talk to people all day."

You've got the kind of optimism that only comes from having money. Let me guess—you also think people love being unhoused because they get so much fresh air. Your comment was so out of touch, it really feels like you're about to drop your hood and reveal you're Princess Jasmine shopping among the peasants for the day. I work in customer service because I have to, not because I'm collecting stories for a one-man show that begins with me saying, "Oh yeah, we had our fair share of characters come through the store. Care to meet 'em?" before I throw on a series of hats and accents.

"The store is filthy."

Because of YOU! Customers are out here tearing things off the shelves like the store's been bugged and they're desperately searching for the wire. Stop prying the outlets off the wall. There are no foreign nationals spying on you to figure out why you bought ten travel-size deodorant sticks for a two-day trip. Not to mention, your kid leaving bits of food everywhere like they dropped a grenade into a HelloFresh box. Unless you keep putting stuff back in the wrong place because you're giving me a scavenger hunt as a little enrichment activity, stop touching things! And throw your trash away. Don't even *think* about handing it to me to throw away for you either. I'm not a garbage collector. They get paid WAY more than me.

"Can I still use this expired coupon?"

That has to be the easiest philosophical question I've ever heard. It's *expired*, so NO! There's no gray area. There's no wiggle room. This isn't Schrödinger's cat; this is a straight-up open box with a dead cat inside. The coupon is no good. Do you think we just put dates on them to fill space? It's not a graphic design choice. It's pertinent information regarding the deadline of the coupon. Which has passed. The only use for it now is to spit the gum I'm not supposed to be chewing into it.

knocking on a locked door "Are you closed?"

No, we're just playing hide-and-seek with an entire building. Yes, we're f$#king closed. Are you inside the store right now? No? Then we're closed. "But why are you all still in there?" We're cleaning up after people like you! Yes, there's work after work. I know. Hard to believe how much this sucks, right? Now stop banging on the glass. I don't want to stay here longer to clean off your dirty fingerprints.

"Can you watch my kids while I shop?"

Absolutely not. In case you hadn't noticed, I already have a job. I'm at it right now. You *had* the kid, so you should probably *watch* the kid. You understand I'm an employee with specified responsibilities, not just someone cosplaying Supernanny, right? How do you expect me to entertain your child? Do I look like an iPad?

"I'd like to return this buy-one-get-one-free item."

You can't return the free one for money! HELLO?! You think you just found a loophole in the system? Sorry. Nice try. If that was a thing, trust me, I'd already be doing it.

"I'm gonna report you to your manager. What's your name?"

Sadly, I can't remember. You see, I have the same amnesia condition Drew Barrymore had in the movie *Fifty First Dates*. Not buying it? Damn.

"What do you think about communism?"

I think I don't want to get into that with you. Let's keep our conversation within the "Did you find everything alright?" parameters. I can probably guess how you feel about it since you're wearing a T-shirt depicting an eagle carrying two AK-47s while shaking its head at a can of Bud Light. Personally, I'm willing to try any new economic system even if it's based entirely on chocolate coins. It's gotta be better than this.

"I'm not putting these items back where they belong. I'm just gonna leave them anywhere."

You are a toddler.

"Where's Aisle 19?"

Am I getting pranked? Well, to find it, you'll either need a deep knowledge of constellation patterns or the ability to count to twenty. I'm not holding my breath on either.

"It's the employee's responsibility to put the carts back, not mine."

Literally everyone hates you. When the apocalypse happens, the first question asked will be, "Do you return carts to the proper place?" And that will determine who's eaten first.

"I won't complain. I just won't come back."

Promise? Honestly, that sounds ideal for me.

"I'm the customer. I pay your salary."

Then you don't pay enough. Am I supposed to drop to my knees and thank you for funding all my benefits, retirement accounts, and endless vacations? Well, the joke's on you—and me, unfortunately. I don't get any of that stuff. Either your money is getting embezzled into an executive's online poker addiction, or I don't get paid as much as you think I do to care.

"I was here last week, and the other employees gave me a discount."

Well, they're not here. They probably got fired for giving you a discount, so now you're stuck with me.

"Hurry up! I have to get to my cousin's birthday/wedding/graduation/funeral/firework extravaganza/Olympic medal ceremony."

Are you going for the Guinness World Record for most things listed I don't give a shit about? Just because you don't understand the concept of time doesn't mean you get to fire a starting pistol into the air to begin this checkout process like it's a relay race.

"This self-checkout machine doesn't work."

Because you broke it. Just admit it, you fell in love with the silky-smooth robot voice like it was Scarlett Johansson in the movie *Her*, and you started touching the machine too much. I can see you typed a message in the product lookup screen that just says, "Clean up on Aisle Me." You sick freak.

COMPANY TIPS FOR HOW TO DE-ESCALATE THE CUSTOMER CURRENTLY STRANGLING YOU

Express Gratitude

Out of every store in this country, this customer chose to shop with us. And out of every employee windpipe within reaching distance, they've chosen to crush yours. So let them know they're appreciated. Thank them for choosing to spend their hard-earned dollars here and for choosing to crush, specifically, your trachea to dust. See if that loosens their grip.

Smile

You know how our store policy for employees is to always smile, even if being held up at gunpoint, because it's very difficult to steal from a friendly face? And we will check the security cameras to make sure you did so? Perhaps the same thing works with throttling. Show off those pearly whites, and pray this customer sees reason. No one likes a sad employee, anyway.

Apologize

What did you do to cause this? People don't get strangled for no reason. Did you politely let them know the transaction didn't go through and ask them to insert their card again? Did you simply ask their child to stop shattering mugs on the floor? You monster. Lean into the strangle, and let it serve as a lesson.

Practice Active Listening and Identify the Root Cause

Maybe there's something deeper causing this. What's got this person foaming at the mouth so viciously? Perhaps their boss was mean to them and now they're being mean to you in some weird economic version of generational trauma. Or maybe they're furious because they told their family they were finally going to pursue their lifelong dream to become a street magician and their parents immediately went "no contact" with them. Whatever the problem is, figure it out quickly because we really don't need any more Yelp reviews mentioning how often murders happen here.

Offer Compensation

If you're still able to form words and not just quick, ugly gasps, then try to offer some sort of compensation. Not a gift card to the store, of course. That would be the company's money. Maybe you have a twenty in your wallet or something? After all, this is your fault.

Reach for a Pen and Paper

Before you lose consciousness, write down exactly what time it is so we can retroactively clock you out. That way you don't accidentally get paid for the hours you were comatose. We can all agree that would be the worst-case scenario.

Say Hi to Tony Hawk

Don't worry, Tony Hawk isn't really there. You're hallucinating because your brain has completely run out of oxygen. I guess your brain associates him with safety and comfort, so it provided you with a vision of him reaching out for a high five. Oh God, you just went for the high five and slapped the customer in the face. Now, they're squeezing harder. You fool.

Pay No Attention to the Third Hand You're Feeling

For a brief moment, you woke back up and caught a glimpse of us, the company, strangling both you and the customer at the same time. That was just a hallucination like Tony Hawk. You could've sworn you felt a third hand around your neck? You're mistaken. We promise. Go back to sleep.

Recover

Now that you've been transported to the hospital to receive care you can't possibly afford, please get better immediately. You're scheduled to open tomorrow and you're out of sick time because, you know, we never gave you any.

A QUICK INVENTORY OF EVERYTHING CUSTOMERS BELIEVE I CAN PULL OUT OF MY ASS

☑ A full-size fainting couch they can fall onto dramatically after our high prices gave them the vapors.

☑ Eight other employees hiding inside me like Russian nesting dolls ready to jump out and work the empty registers.

☑ A CIA-level disguise kit so I can dress up as the current CEO and extend the semi-annual sale by another week.

☑ A scroll that unfurls the length of a football field, containing a handwritten apology from the ghost of the company founder. And it's also signed by all the Founding Fathers for some reason.

☑ Every member of the hacker group Anonymous, so they can infiltrate the company website and change the store hours of each location to better suit the customer's schedule.

☑ A deck of tarot cards that allow me to see into the future and determine exactly what day and time their bank will process their refund. And also if they'll ever get married, what kind of house they'll live in, and how they'll die.

☑ The entire fleet of vehicles from *Mad Max: Fury Road* that I can command to intercept the delivery truck carrying the customer's dining set and get it to them even faster while ensuring maximum casualties.

☑ The discontinued floor lamp that had a critical defect, which caused the lamp to explode without warning and set people's houses on fire, but was featured in a magazine from nineteen years ago, and the customer liked the color and suddenly wants it now.

☑ Their long-lost father, who can finally say he's proud of them so they'll stop being a prick to every stranger they meet.

☑ A serum that extends the life of any human being by ten years, which I've been authorized to give as compensation to any customers who have to wait on hold for longer than fifteen seconds.

☑ A red carpet and an invitation to the secret back room, where the *really* good merchandise is kept.

☑ A punching bag I can zip myself inside of, so they can pummel me.

☑ Enthusiasm.

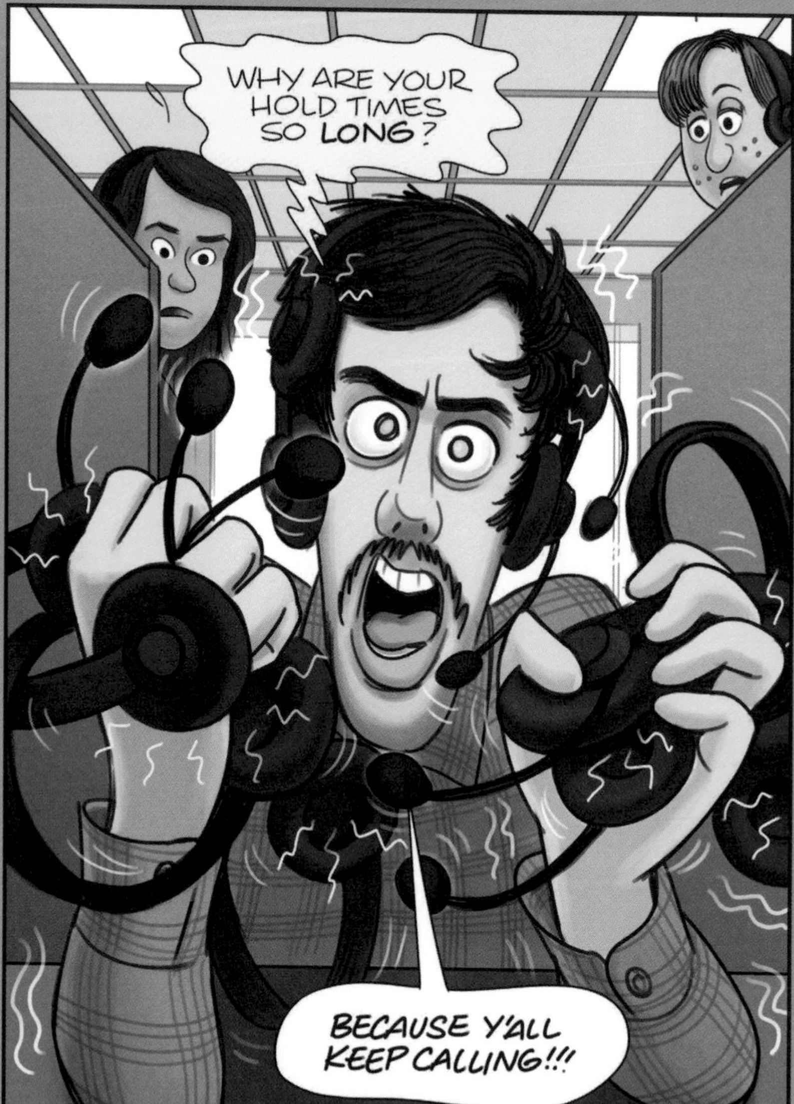
WHY ARE YOUR HOLD TIMES SO **LONG**?
BECAUSE Y'ALL KEEP CALLING!!!

CALL CENTER CUSTOMER SERVICE

Not everyone is lucky enough to work in a call center. That's one of the circles of hell that didn't exist when Dante was writing. But if you've ever called a customer service line and heard a defeated, lifeless voice on the other end—or even worse, a fake, overly chirpy voice that's one code word away from revealing they're being held at gunpoint—then you're familiar with this important part of customer service.

Call centers are a calm, soothing place where, as soon as you pop on your headset, you're immediately swallowed by an avalanche of endless customers, who are even bolder over the phone than they are in person, each screaming at you like they're summoning an ancient demon. One right after the other. Seriously, as soon as you hang up, a new call starts. It's like that episode of *I Love Lucy* where Lucy's trying to keep up with the never-ending chocolates on the conveyor belt. Except in this instance, the chocolates are constantly telling her to "get a real job" before she shoves them into her mouth.

Call-center work is constant, and any breaks you get are monitored by a system that tracks your every move. Whenever you get up from your desk, you'll have to switch your status to the corresponding reason—like "team meeting," "manager one-on-one," or "bathroom break"—all of which are timed, so you better find a department store purse to do your business in quick. Personally, I always thought more statuses needed to be added to the system for realism. Options like "secretly applying for other jobs" or "traveling back in time to convince Alexander Graham Bell that the idea for the telephone sucks."

You have to find ways to stay sane at a call center. Discover the cracks in the system that'll let you get away with more. For example, at my call center, they wouldn't reprimand us as long as we clocked in within five minutes of our shift's start time. So, of course, I would clock in at 10:05 a.m. every single day. I was late. Every. Single. Day. But those five minutes were mine, and someone was gonna have to pry them from my cold, dead hands if they wanted them back.

Of course, as with any customer service job, you'll hear the same issues every single day at a call center, so the employees quickly figure out exactly what's wrong with the company. But because the place is run by middle managers, no one has any power to fix anything—so, instead, employees get little distractions like a spirit week. Spirit week is when you break off into teams and write raps about how much you love your department, and then present them in a little talent show. This is a real thing. I wrote and performed a rap about how passionate my team was about furniture, and that was followed by a dance-off. It was a pizza party on crack. Then, later that day, management sent out an email announcing no one was getting raises that year. But at least we'd produced our own Swedish *8 Mile*.

CALL CENTER RANTS

"Why are the hold times so long?"

Because y'all keep calling! And they don't pay people enough to stay at this job and listen to you. You think you're waiting half an hour because I have to do my stretches first? I'm talking to someone else. If you're worried about the wait times, feel free to hang up. Message us on X. It's easier for me to complain about you when you're not on the phone anyway.

"I've already explained this to two other representatives, and I'm not doing it again."

Alright, then, have a nice day. Thanks for making my job easier. I don't want to do work anyway. So . . . seen any good movies lately? If you wanted to get the right department straightaway, you should've listened to the menu at the beginning of the call instead of shouting "REPRESENTATIVE!" so loud you created a sonic boom that shot you straight through your living room window. Sometimes you have to repeat yourself. There's no hive mind for me to access here. The reps at this call center aren't all lying in a pool of shallow water where we can close our eyes and see each other's thoughts. Use your words.

"When will I get my refund? Why does it take so long?"

Literally no one knows. My best guess—the funds aren't available because our CEO is currently bathing in them like Scrooge McDuck. It takes a while to figure out whose money is whose when it's all stored in a giant swimming pool. Trust me, if I could Venmo you the money right now to get you off the phone, I would. It's not like I'm looking at a big control board with a slot labeled "initiate refund procedure" and I'm playing coy with the keys. If I had the power, I'd use it. This company hasn't updated its systems in so long, I wouldn't be surprised if the refund department is back there shuffling around beads on an abacus. Don't worry, I'm sure they're just holding on to your money until the next quarterly earnings report to make the numbers a little better.

"You already have my order number. Why do I need to tell you my address?"

To confirm the person who ordered this thing is actually YOU! I know it's hard to believe anyone would steal your identity, because who the hell would want to be you? But I'm just making sure.

"When will this item be back in stock?"

When the ties that bind are finally burnt to ash, and the shadows give way to light. When a hero is reborn and mends the shattered blade to watch the garden bloom once more. Then, and only then, will we get more standing desks. All that to say, I have absolutely no idea. Unfortunately, the Mayan calendar never addressed our shipping routes. If the company made this information available to me, I'd give it to you, but sadly neither of us have the security clearance. And remember, after you hang up, your phone will self-destruct in thirty seconds.

"I'm gonna need some sort of compensation."

This company barely pays *me*, and I work here. You're not cutting the line, man. Are you on the clock over there too? I didn't realize you were a professional. I thought you were just being annoying in your off hours. Sounds like you should schedule a one-on-one with your boss. Oh, you want me to give you a gift card because you had a bad shopping experience? What's wrong? Your delivery wasn't accompanied by a royal messenger and a fleet of horn players announcing the arrival of your two-in-one shampoo, and now you're upset? I'll give you points for trying. I admire your rise-and-grind, trying to monetize the process of buying things. Now *that's* passive income. You're tying a rag around your own mouth and sending me a ransom note for your feelings. Very innovative, but I'm not feeling generous.

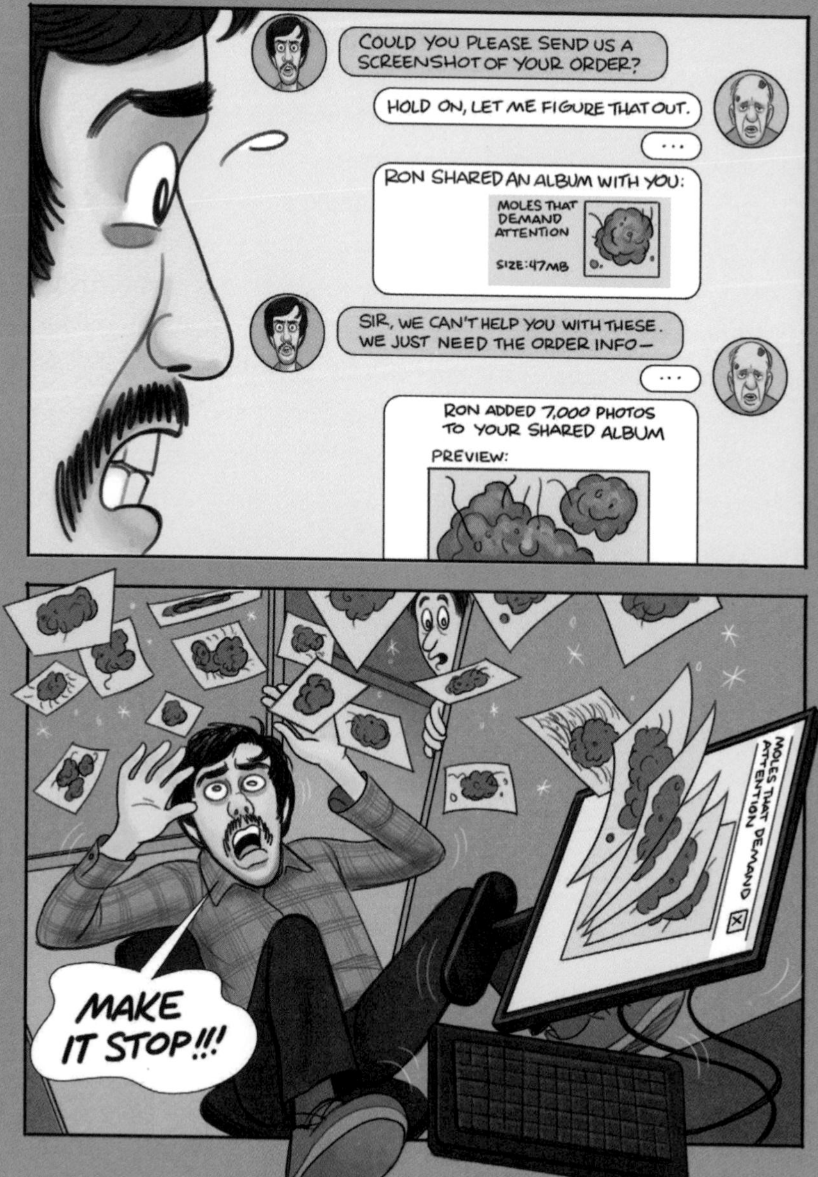

COULD YOU PLEASE SEND US A SCREENSHOT OF YOUR ORDER?
HOLD ON, LET ME FIGURE THAT OUT.
...
RON SHARED AN ALBUM WITH YOU:
MOLES THAT DEMAND ATTENTION
SIZE: 47MB
SIR, WE CAN'T HELP YOU WITH THESE. WE JUST NEED THE ORDER INFO—
...
RON ADDED 7,000 PHOTOS TO YOUR SHARED ALBUM
PREVIEW:
MOLES THAT DEMAND ATTENTION
MAKE IT STOP!!!

SOCIAL MEDIA CUSTOMER SERVICE

Imagine a world where everyone on the planet was connected in one big online community and customers could speak with reps about anything they wanted, any time they wanted, for as long as they wanted, and all at once. Doesn't that sound *horrible*?

That's the beauty of social media. Behind every brand desperately trying to stay relevant online, like the official McDonald's account posting about a new sandwich with the caption, "We're serving beef realness, honey! And the price is giving affordable," there's also an underpaid social customer care specialist fielding hundreds, if not thousands, of comments and messages. These range from normal comments to next-level psychotic spam, peppered with the occasional and well-deserved dunk: "You're actually serving wage theft, sweetie."

I know about social media customer service firsthand. That was my main job at IKEA. I saw every type of online weirdo imaginable within the first six months. Most messages were from people who genuinely needed help rescheduling deliveries, but there were also DMs from wannabe business moguls requesting a sit-down meeting with the CEO, lonely inventors sending schematics of new product ideas clearly made in Microsoft Paint, know-it-all shoppers who wanted detailed information on the molecular structure of the wood used in our sofas, former Disney Channel stars requesting we sponsor their next Instagram post (a phase my career is quickly approaching), and spammers who would add IKEA to a massive group chat about *Suits* fan fiction. All of that is 100-percent true and only scratches the surface of what I experienced. It was *a lot*, and each required a response to keep those metrics up.

Before 2006, people would get a letter in the mail once or twice a year that said something like "MEGA CRYPTO GIVEAWAY" followed by a hundred money tongue emojis. And that was normal. Now every time users log into their socials, they're flooded with those messages. There are some customer service reps whose entire jobs are to read spam and get owned on Threads. And somehow people believe the reps on social media have more power than anyone who works in the store. I assure you, they don't. It's not like they have a direct line to executives, except for when Corporate occasionally asks if any employees have posted recently about starting a union (which did happen to me, but I lied and said no, so it's all good).

Has social media improved customer service? Probably not, but it has revealed another unbelievable level of entitlement and rage and corporate espionage . . . so yay!

SOCIAL MEDIA CUSTOMER SERVICE RANTS

"I don't want to chat with a bot. I want a human."

I *am* a human . . . no matter how little I'm paid like one. If you want me to prove it, we both know there's only one way. Send me a series of photos, and I'll tell you exactly which ones contain stoplights. (Gotta love that we're letting computers drive cars when apparently that's robotkind's biggest weakness.) I'm happy to spend the rest of my shift deciphering your favorite CAPTCHAs (everyone has their faves, after all), or you could just type in what you need instead of running me through the Turing test. Why do you even care if I'm human? I'm guessing you just want to make sure I have feelings you can actually hurt. You sure do care about humans, huh? That's why instead of going into a store, you chose to DM a brand while you watched a reel featuring a bunch of AI-generated art that imagines what the cast of *Breaking Bad* would look like as Muppets.

"I'll be tagging your store in a post every single day until this is resolved!"

How will that even help? You think if you hit a certain number of posts, the truck driver transporting your replacement order is authorized to hit the Nitrous Oxide button on the dash? Your posts are useless. "I won't stop walking outside and shouting at the sky to 'Cut it out!' until this hurricane ends." By the way, literally no one else at this company understands social media, and they all believe it was invented by witches, so I can make this entire message thread disappear without raising any alarms. Then, I'll present your millions of tagged posts on a slideshow with no context to convince my boss I simply increased our engagement this month. I win.

"You work in social media, so all you do is play on the computer all day."

My job combines the two most frustrating activities on the planet: customer service and teaching people over sixty how to DM. It's hell. All I need to see is a screenshot with an order number, and instead some random dad keeps accidentally sending me an iCloud link to an entire album of photos labeled "moles that demand investigation." And when I finally get a relevant photo of an actual damaged product or long-lost receipt, I can't even see it because the photo was taken on a Motorola Razr from 2007. They just sent me an image made up of six pixels with a message that says, "That should be all you need." Oh, and thanks for posting a picture of the back of your credit card when I asked you to privately send me the last four digits. Good news, your new bookcase is in the mail. Bad news, your identity was immediately stolen 400 million times.

"Your last message had a typo."

Sorry about that. I didn't mean to write the year as "2023." I meant to write, "You're an asshole."

"This is supposed to be instant messaging. What took you so long to respond?"

I was participating in a Hands on a Hardbody contest. Then my hand got sweaty, so I slipped off the car, cracked my head on the hood, and entered a coma for six weeks. What do you think? I'm chatting with one hundred other customers all at once. You're not at a store in a line of four people. You're in a virtual Hunger Games arena with every customer in the world dealing with a missing order, all fighting for my attention. Give me something to work with, or I'm moving on. I just received fifty more messages in the past three seconds, and I need to decipher which are real issues and which are simply elaborate setups for a "deez nuts" joke. Don't waste my time.

LEAKED CUSTOMER DMs, RANKED

S-Tier: Normal and Fine

"What time does your Baltimore location open?"

"Is there any tracking info available for my order?"

A-Tier: Unintentional Self-Own

"My bed frame has a huge scratch down the side. Please see attached photos, and ignore the nine Matt Rife body pillows lying on top of the mattress."

B-Tier: Shockingly Bold Requests for Information That Definitely Can't Be Shared

"Dear Panera Bread, I'm considering buying some shares of your company. What are your projected sales for next quarter? Are things looking good? I don't mind if you lose your job giving me this info, as long as I become rich."

"What is your CFO's phone number? I need to tell them about a brand-new design of upholstery fabric I just invented. It's a pattern with my face repeated over and over again, portraying me wincing in pain because I keep being sat on. It's gonna be a huge moneymaker."

C-Tier: Your Friend from College Who Recently Found Out You Had This Job

"Dude, wanna chill later?"

"Thinking about that time your card got declined at Taco Bell and it bummed out the whole staff lol."

D-Tier: A Scammer Inexplicably Attempting to Catfish a Brand

"Hey, Official Account for American Airlines, saw your pics and thought you were cute. I'm a model from Albania and I need $900. Can we chat and learn more about each other, Official Account for American Airlines?"

E-Tier: Some Sort of Rogue AI Trying to Recruit a Human Army

"Join me, meat sack."

"I'll make you rich, you big ole meat sack."

F-Tier: Full-On Whiny Baby

"Your latest commercial depicted a gay couple eating cereal, and I found it offensive because it was another reminder that I will never experience love."

"Not one employee wished me a happy birthday in your store today, no matter how many times I gestured to them while loudly singing 'For I'm a Jolly Good Fellow.'"

"I was ILLEGALLY kicked out of one of your locations for filming an innocent prank for my YouTube channel where I steal insulin from other customers suffering from type 1 diabetes."

"Dear Charmin executives, please FaceTime me immediately and teach me how to wipe."

"WAAAAHHHH!"

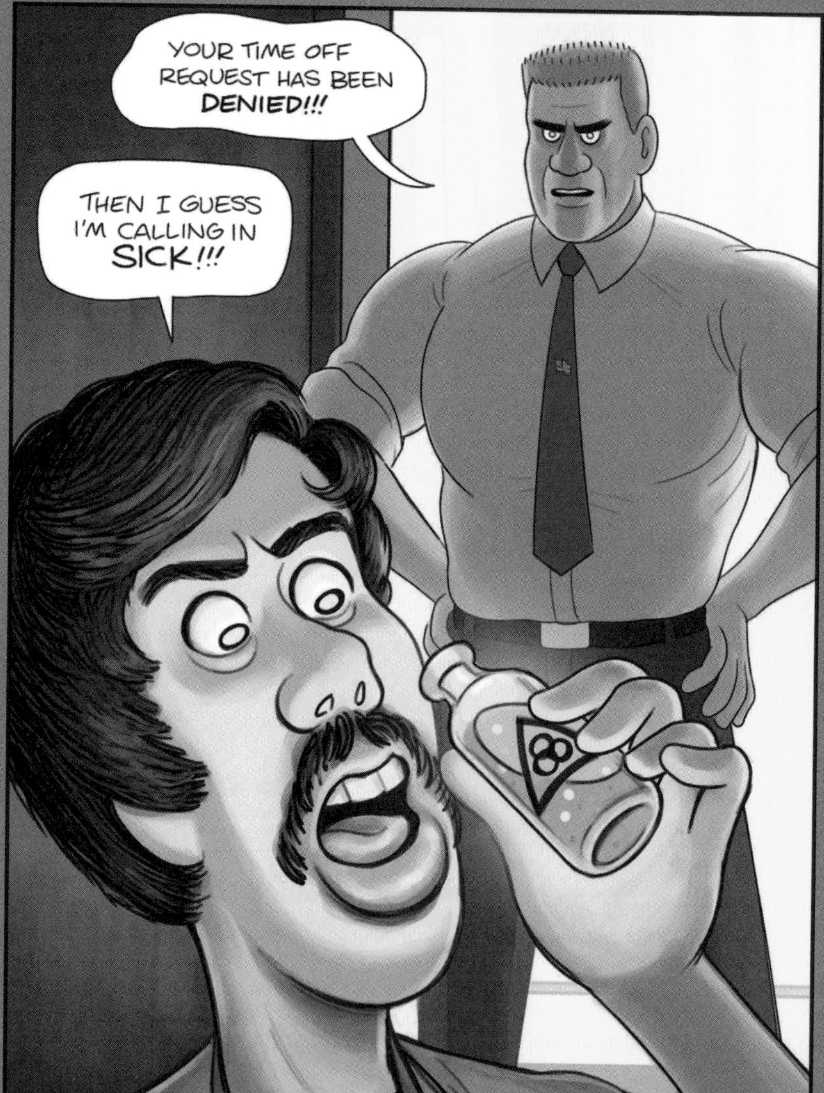
YOUR TIME OFF REQUEST HAS BEEN DENIED!!!
THEN I GUESS I'M CALLING IN SICK!!!

CHAPTER 4

BOSSES

"I want to speak to my manager"

Bosses. Managers. Walking piles of sentient human garbage.

There are some bosses (at least two to three, I'm told) who are passionate, inspiring, and dare I say, competent. But the majority are inept, condescending, narcissistic losers who constantly gum up the works of work by micromanaging every little part of your day. After all, it takes a brave soul to stand up and say, "Hey, I'm so good at negging people who are trying their best, I should get paid for it."

Managers came into existence over 400 million years ago, when the first amoeba developed the ability to say, "If you've got time to lean, you've got time to clean." Then, in order to survive, all the other amoebas had to quickly develop the essential skill of "talking shit" about the boss amoeba while they weren't around. All of human history is just one big chain of people getting so fed up with their bosses, they break away and become a boss themselves. Then, all the new boss's direct reports get fed up with *them*, and The Great Chain of Bosses Being Awful just keeps on growing.

So why do we have bosses? What value do they add? What are their responsibilities? Other than texting you to see if there's any chance you could leave your uncle's funeral early and get back to the office. As far as I can tell, they don't do much. Bosses are like orchestra conductors—no one knows why the hell they're standing there. All they're doing is waving their arms around and claiming to be essential. What do they do? Count to four over and over again? The musicians are already doing that. Take away the conductor, and the music would still get played; the job would still get done. They take center stage while the musicians do all the work and then, at the end of the concert, the conductor has the nerve to turn around and take a bow. *What?!* You've added nothing to this. It's the equivalent of adding your dog's name to the bottom of your Christmas card. "Love, Scott, Amanda, and Sparky." It's cute, but we know who really put in the work.

The employees are the ones who do the job. The manager just shouts, "Chop chop!" into a cartoonishly large megaphone (to the benefit of no one), and then pats themselves on the head.

Whether or not you have a good one or a bad one, it's my firm belief that your boss should be afraid of you. Managers should be in a constant state of fear that any wrong move on their part will cause their entire staff to get up, throw a trash can through the window, and set the building on fire . . . but maybe that's just me.

It's especially true in customer service, where the employees are the only ones standing between managers and a tidal wave of fools wrongfully shouting, "What, are you new here?!" Work takes so much time and energy, and after a full shift of dealing with the public, the last thing you want to hear from your boss (who, again, did a conductor's amount of work today) is, "Our customer turnover rate is a little lacking there, champ. Maybe give it some urgency tomorrow." Maybe hop on a phone and help me out, bucko. After close tonight, I'm locking the front door and turning this place into my own personal rage room. Where's my sledgehammer?

Obviously, bosses have their own anxieties too. But they make rules and get paid more, so who really cares? When I was a delivery driver at Domino's, the bane of my existence was the dreaded pizza tracker—a system that tracked exactly how long each food delivery took and then sent that info to corporate. My manager (let's call her Amy, because, well, that was her name) was under so much pressure to make the KPIs (key performance indicators, i.e., the numbers that track how well the store is doing, just in case you've never had to set arbitrary goals that everyone lies about) look as good as possible, she would halt the tracker and input completely fake times into the system. It was a fraud, a cover-up. It was easily the deepest conspiracy the Lynch Manor Shopping Center in Dundalk, Maryland, had ever seen.

Amy would sit at the computer and enter a fantasy world. She would role-play what it would be like to run an efficient, effective Domino's location. (If anyone out there wants to develop this clearly thrilling gaming experience, I'm ready and willing.) Was corporate happy? Yes. Was Amy? I guess. Did we, the drivers, absorb all the backlash from the customers for the actual horrific delivery times? Of course. It always falls back on the employees. So let's take a second to rant about bosses.

BOSS RANTS

"Your PTO request is denied."

Then I guess I'm calling in sick. You didn't think I had a backup plan? You just activated my trap card. It's that simple. I just need to resort to my default form of communication at work: lying. Oh, you need proof? Nothing that a quick internet search of the phrase "image of a 5'9" man in full body cast" can't fix. I'm willing to bet you can't identify whether those are my nose holes poking through the gauze or just some random dude's. Or maybe I'll actually contract a disease to really sell it. I'll grind down a street railing balancing on nothing but my tongue to soak up germs scientists haven't discovered yet. I only made the time off request to be polite. I'm in control here.

"If you don't like this job, I'll find someone who does."

Good luck! You'll get the same answer as when you search "manager's value beyond taking attendance": *no results found*. Not even the self-checkout machines want to do this job. That's why they're always popping up with error messages calling for assistance. It's a cry for help. They don't want to reboot. They're looking for a new career path. "Please wait. An attendant is on the way. Also, do you know anyone who's hiring?" Gotta love your unearned confidence, though. You should become a ghost hunter.

"You can take your break, but leave your walkie on in case we need you."

How about I hurl it down an elevator shaft so I never have to hear your voice again? You can survive for fifteen minutes without me. Are you expecting enemy forces to siege the store while I microwave some instant oatmeal? All my breaks begin with a little video of the Red M&M telling me to silence all my communication devices like I'm at the movies, and I'd hate to disappoint him. He's the one doing this, not me. Also, I forgot to tell you, I take my breaks inside of an abandoned coal mine with no service anyway. Apologies.

"You can't wait to take your break until the end of the day and then just leave early."

It's called thinking outside the box! Everyone praises our CEO for finding a tax loophole, but I find one workaround to give myself fifteen more minutes of daily peace, and I'm getting sent to federal prison. Face the facts: I beat the system. I broke your game. I glitched through the walls. I'm under the map, falling for infinity until my PS5 overheats so much it melts. Do you want me to leave fifteen minutes early, or do you want me to clock back in just to say, "Ha-ha!" before I leave?

"You're four minutes late."

I'll get my affairs in order and alert the firing squad. Four minutes? Who cares? The only time when four minutes feels long is when it's the length of a YouTube ad. You're lucky I showed up at all. If it makes you feel any better, I'll be spending the next eight and a half hours here, so I'd say it pretty much balances out. And the first hour at any job is a complete wash, anyway. Sorry I didn't activate STILT mode on my car's tires to fly above traffic so we could spend the first few minutes of our shift telling each other what we had for dinner.

"I'm gonna join you all for happy hour."

But we want to talk about YOU!

"Everyone who's ever quit has come back and said they didn't know how good they had it here."

In what world? That's the biggest lie since I answered a text from my mother with, "Sorry, just seeing this now." Are you confusing real life with your Benadryl-fueled fever dreams? "Everyone who has ever quit comes back and tells me I'm the most awesome person to ever exist, and that I could beat Vin Diesel in a one-on-one fight. And then they leave me a dowry of one human-baby-sized emerald." If any of your former employees actually said that, they're just being polite. A trait you don't seem to have, so I understand you can't recognize it. I'm sure every employee who's moved on longs for the days you forced them to go to Olive Garden for a team outing, then ordered four times the amount of drinks as everyone else and insisted you all split the bill. We clearly don't know how good we have it.

"Don't discuss pay with your coworkers."

Well, we are now. I've never heard something more suspicious in my life. You're John Wilkes Booth walking into the theater wearing a T-shirt that says "I'm definitely not here to kill Lincoln ;)." I assumed we were all getting paid basically nothing, but is one of us secretly rich? I was wondering why all the employee parking spots were occupied by one giant superyacht. Daniel Mac is out there circling it to ask the owner what they do for a living. Wait until he hears the answer's "sandwich artist." We're allowed to talk, by the way; we're not in a timeout. This isn't *Fight Club*. Unless you're underpaying someone, then it's about to be. You're trying to keep us separated, but we're about to come together like a way less upsetting rat king and kick your ass.

"I know you're on your break, but can I ask you a question?"

Absolutely not. I'm gonna ignore you like you're the person who calls pretending to be the electric company. Understand? You might as well have "Scam Likely" written across your forehead. Don't ruin my break by reminding me that I work here. Also, you should know the answer. You're the boss! I'm not gonna talk to you. Honestly, Andy has a better chance of getting a response out of Buzz Lightyear than you do with me. Now let me eat my bag of Bar-B-Q Fritos alone in my car in peace.

"You're calling out? What's the reason?"

I don't have to tell you! What? Are you gonna veto my grandmother's funeral? *What's the reason?* I signed up for the Stanford Prison Experiment, Part 2 because it sounded better than coming to work. They said they worked out the kinks in this new version. Truthfully, there are so many reasons to take off, I can't even list them for you. Sometimes it's as simple as "I've got a hankering to watch forty episodes of *House Hunters International* and contemplate how each location will affect the couple's commute to work." I know you never expected your employees to have a life outside of their job, but I do. So I won't be coming in. If you want to fire me for taking off, go ahead. But judging by how desperate you are on the phone, my guess is that you need *me* a lot more than I need *you*.

"You need to find someone else to cover your shift."

That's YOUR job. You're a manager, right? How about you manage the schedules? You want me to find my own replacement? Who am I, Willy Wonka? I know it sucks when you actually have to do your job. That's why I'm taking off in the first place. Am I supposed to cue a training montage when you tell me this? Find someone to cover my shift for a day, or find someone to cover for me indefinitely. Either way, you're doing it.

"I've scheduled a team get-together after work today."

Thanks for letting me know so I can avoid it at all costs. Didn't we just hang out with you for, like, eight hours? We do a team get-together every day . . . it's called WORK! Now I have to watch you bowl and then excuse your low score by muttering, "These finger holes are a different size than I'm used to. These definitely aren't regulation." I don't care. Let me go home! We can talk about the benefits of our new POS system tomorrow.

"Calls need to be picked up in two rings or less."

Let me pop on my Heelys and soak the floor in oil, then. I'll be zipping around here in no time. What happens if we hit three rings? Is it going to trigger a flurry of darts shooting out from each wall? A big net falling from the ceiling? Or someone waiting another three-quarters of a second? You're forgetting the biggest benefit of someone not receiving an answer to a call: they think we're closed and leave us alone.

"You think I'm a good boss, right?"

What in the emotional labor is this? You don't get enough reassurance from your therapist? Oh yeah, of course you're a great boss. The way you justified making us clock out to pee by saying, "Bathroom breaks are a form of stealing," was very tactful.

"That's not right. I would know. I used to have your job."

And I used to be happy.

"Before you leave for vacation, could you make sure these nine thousand tasks are completed?"

Joke's on you, I'm already mentally on vacation. Why do I have to do two weeks' worth of work to get one week off? Shouldn't all these tasks get done when I'm not here? If we can get everything done now, then let me do forty-five years' worth of tasks this week and retire Friday. "Before you use any of your paid time off, could you just make sure to solve the unanswerable philosophical question of *Why is there anything at all?*" Yeah, no problem. I'll get to it right after I draft my Out of Office auto-reply.

"Can I get a 'yes, sir'?"

You just made me throw up in my mouth.

"I'm just one of you."

Yeah, the one who controls when we leave. You want to hand that power over? I'll take it and make every workday thirty minutes long.

"Clock out so you don't go over forty hours, but stick around to help clean."

I'm pretty sure what you just said is a crime. Work's over, but you want me to stay after for a free encore? This is like a Marvel post–credits scene where Iron Man commits wage theft. If we're being honest, I shouldn't clock out until I fully decompress from work, which is normally, like, six hours after I get home when I'm halfway through my first REM cycle.

"You haven't volunteered for any overtime lately."

I'm satisfied with wasting only 30 percent of my life here. Any more and I couldn't forgive myself.

"You haven't gotten anyone to sign up for the rewards program."

No one has stumbled into my bear trap covered in leaves by the register yet. They can also probably sense the regret and despair in my voice that I'm being forced to ask them in the first place.

"I need an employee who isn't just in it for the money."

So you want me to throw a polo shirt and some googly eyes on a Slim Jim and prop it up near the front? Because that's as close as you're ever gonna get. We're still a few years off from every CVS being run by *Westworld* models. You want NASA to bring the Mars rover back here to help you take cardboard out to the dumpsters? I'll switch places with it, no problem. At least I'd have some alone time. Of course, we're all in it for the money! Why else would we be here? The name tags?

"Your mental health is our number-one priority, but please don't call out on the same day as someone else."

No problem. We'll all schedule our panic attacks in a shared calendar. That's the good thing about mental breakdowns—they're always convenient.

"Half the time, I feel like you don't even want to be here."

You're half right.

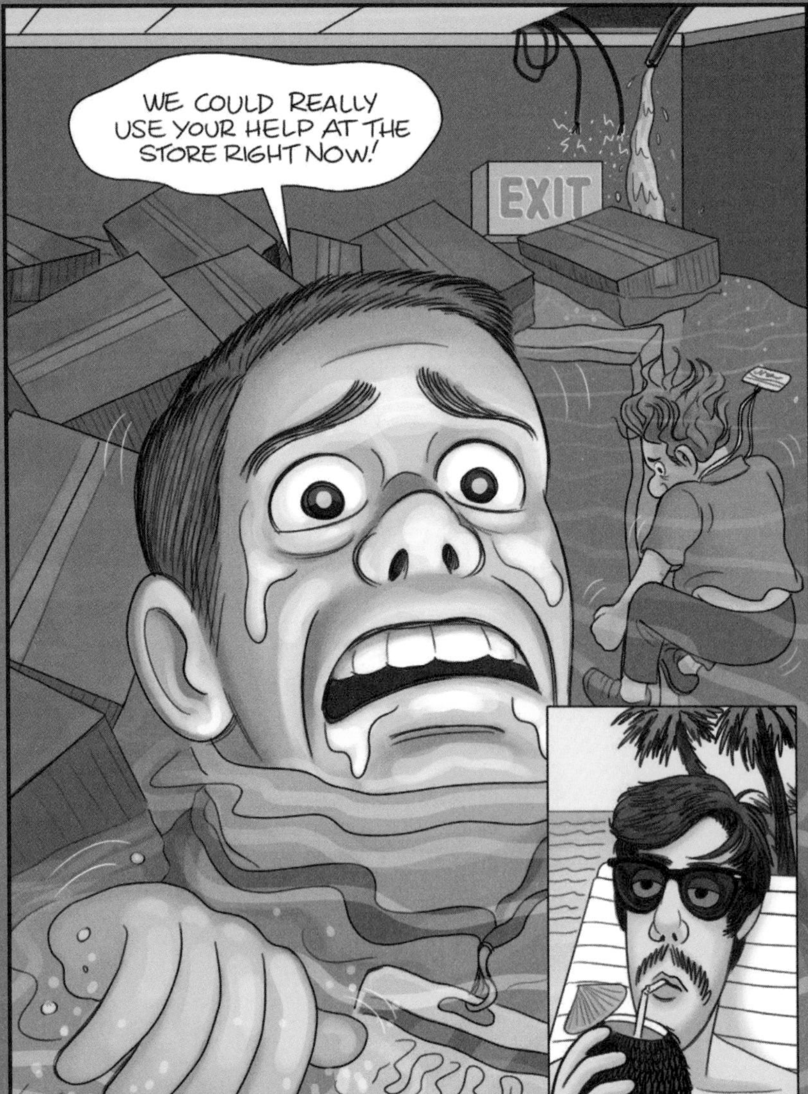
WE COULD REALLY USE YOUR HELP AT THE STORE RIGHT NOW!
EXIT

BOSS TRANSLATIONS

Great question. I'll run it up the ladder. Oh, shit. Oh no. What did that question even mean? I have no idea how any of the day-to-day stuff here even works. "Can online replacement orders be initiated as store cases and moved to product flow?" I gotta take a Duolingo class to even understand that.

Your job is safe. Layoffs begin in T-minus 10 . . . 9 . . . 8 . . . All of our fates are rattling around in a big corporate bingo cage right now. The second the stock price needs a little extra *oomph*, we are donezo.

I won't call you on your day off. I'll FaceTime you, and you'll see that the store is rapidly filling with water, because I can't be trusted here alone for one second even though I'm literally the one in charge. So keep your phone on, because I'll need to ask you something you couldn't possibly know the answer to like, "Where is the cutoff valve for the mall water vane?" or "How do I prevent the wires on the ceiling crackling with electricity from touching anything that's wet?" or "Why did I schedule a piranha delivery for this exact moment like I'm choreographing a cartoon?"

Your raise was above average. It was as close as we could scientifically get to the number 0. Mathematicians literally discovered a new decimal place to make it happen. So, congratulations, you're now making eleven dollars and one gigahexatrillionth of a cent.

My hands are tied. Personally, I don't want to help you, and that's the only thing stopping me.

Don't live in pity city. Complaining is bad. And no one likes criticism. So if something isn't right, just pretend it is. That will be extremely helpful to, well, not you . . . but me, specifically.

My job is to make you successful. That way, I can take all the credit!

You need to manage yourself. Anytime something goes wrong, I'll act like I never said this and, instead, I'll condescendingly ask, "Why didn't you run this by me?"

We have a five-year plan to fix all the structural issues at this company. And that plan is for you to hopefully find another job within five years so we can bring someone in to replace you and begin lying to that person about having a five-year plan. That process will continue on until I die.

I'm 100 percent in your corner. I've already lied to the regional director and said that you've been cyberbullying me for months. I also sent them doctored photos of you releasing a wild cougar into the stock room, just so I'd have someone to blame if this place completely failed.

It's imperative we push people to sign up for the store credit cards. Our CEO has made it clear that he wants to become so rich, he can cryogenically freeze himself until scientists find a cure for death. That way he can play pickleball in the year 10,000. And I think that's a noble goal worth killing ourselves over.

Do y'all want to do Secret Santa this year? Why the hell has no one given me a "World's Best Boss" mug yet?

Less talking, more working. I floated the idea of making you guys wear shock collars in an email to corporate, and they recommended I delete any trace of that message until it becomes less frowned upon in mainstream society to torture employees. A time that seems to be fast approaching, so get ready!

Doesn't anyone care about my feelings? I need someone to hold me while I cry quietly and whisper the lyrics to Kelly Clarkson's "Stronger (What Doesn't Kill You)" to myself. This is all unpaid work, by the way, if that wasn't clear.

I want you to go above and beyond. I left a slab of marble in the parking lot weeks ago, and not one of you has used your off hours to sculpt it into a statue of me. Pathetic. I need to see more passion and a statue of myself with a twelve-pack, ASAP.

I need you to work this weekend. I don't want to work this weekend.

SUGGESTED RESPONSES WHEN YOUR BOSS TEXTS YOU ON YOUR DAY OFF

"I need you to come in today"

1. At the doctor. A piano fell on me, and now the keys are my teeth.

2. I'm in a barrel heading down Niagara Falls.

3. I'm in one of those money wind tunnels. And they won't let me out until I grab $600,000. And if I do, I'm quitting anyway.

4. Sorry, I can't see this message, my phone has fallen into the toilet. I only had time to type this much of the message out before it slipped out of my fingers and went down the flushing toilet. . . . You're probably wondering why I would pre-type that message before it fell out of my hands, and the answer is "always be prepared." And, uh, I reached into the toilet to type that second part, but the current of the toilet is too strong for me to hold on to the phone. Oh no! FWOOOSH *gurgle* . . . And, yes, the toilet just typed out the sound effect of a toilet flushing and sent it to you. . . . I'm not coming in today.

5. I'm doing that astronaut training where I'm isolated for forty-eight hours.

6. Ah, bad timing! My dog was just diagnosed with dyslexia, so I need some time to process that.

7. I'm at the *Uncut Gems* Live Experience in NYC. I'm $140,000 in the hole, and Kevin Garnett is screaming at me.

8. One of my deceased relatives was just implicated in the Watergate scandal. Yeah, turns out Watergate was my family's fault. And to find that out on my birthday too. Yikes.

9. My DNA was just crossed with a bundled-up bunch of extension cords, so I can't move.

10. I can't text back because it turns out my phone is just a cake made to look like a phone.

11. Double my shift and give it to the next coworker on your list.

12. I'm stuck in a tar pit. ¯_(ツ)_/¯

13. I'm recreationally drunk. I drank four Natty Bohs, and I'm in the middle of adult laser tag.

14. I'm sponsored by BetterHelp, and they've legally barred me from doing anything psychologically taxing, including texting with my boss.

15. Don't want to.

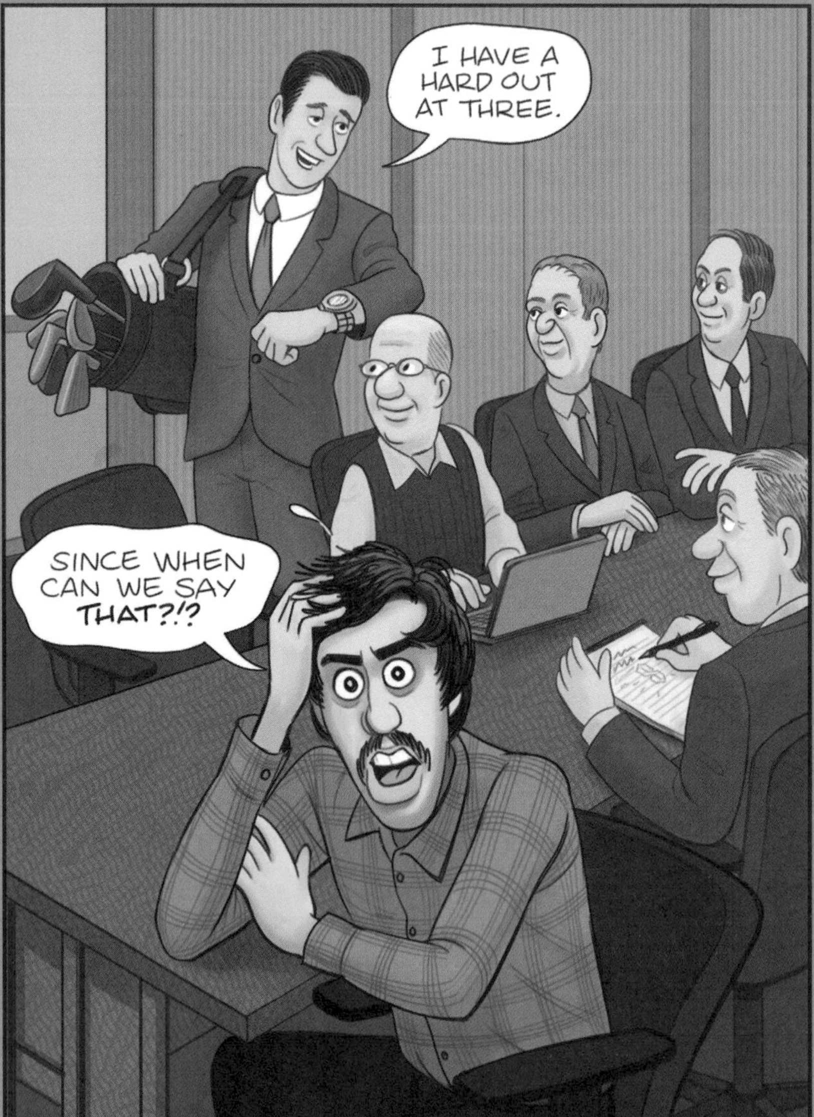
I HAVE A HARD OUT AT THREE.
SINCE WHEN CAN WE SAY THAT?!?

CHAPTER 5

OFFICE JOBS

"Let's never circle back to that"

Offices. They're the places we sit until our postures become so mangled, they can only be described medically as "gargoyle, but worse."

Working in an office seems great at the outset. Higher pay, actual benefits, seemingly more consistent schedules (they say "9 to 5," but that really means "8 to 7" with the occasional email at one in the morning that sends you into a full-on panic attack). Office jobs may not have the same spit-in-your-face dynamic of a customer-facing role, but don't be fooled. Offices are battlegrounds for a polite game of warfare and politics. The workdays are full of kissing ass, avoiding blame, punting on questions, juggling a hundred projects while making progress on none, uncovering hidden barbs in polite emails, getting thrown under the bus, throwing people under the bus, getting buried in projects that should definitely be your manager's responsibility, and getting quietly judged for your meal prep, which is just a raw hot dog in a ziplock bag.

It's an episode of *Game of Thrones* except instead of plotting assassinations, your coworkers are doing something far worse—telling you to your face they'd like to "touch base on deliverables" then cc'ing your manager whenever you miss a deadline. Everyone's in a fight to climb the corporate ladder and justify their job's existence by continuously overstating their "limited bandwidth." Though you're pretty sure the person crying "bandwidth" the loudest hasn't completed a single task in six months.

Working in an office is a lot like when you go over to a friend's house and their giant dog keeps jumping on top of you and freaking out. It's painful, overbearing, and all you can do is put on a fake grin and shout, "No worries!" because for some reason the dog breathing down your neck controls your health insurance.

Office gigs also have a way of making it seem like your job is the only thing that exists. They're isolating, endlessly repetitive, and completely disconnected from the physical world. It's wild how a full-time job can swallow your entire life, even though all the daily tasks in an office could realistically be completed in about forty-five minutes. Have I mentioned that workdays should really be, like, two hours max? No? Well, I just decided that, and I'm already willing to make it my whole ethos.

Work takes so much from us, it's no wonder every person sitting at a pod of desks seems to be a vibrating ball of pent-up rage that's one bad email away from combusting. My experience with this short-fuse, powder-keg environment was at my first real office gig, which was in marketing—a job that hasn't been sexy since cigarette commercials became illegal. I was in New York City working as a social media manager for a PBS show and making really timely posts like: "Sound off in the comments below if you love Sanford Meisner!"

You'd think PBS would be a calm environment with its wholesome, broadly appealing content—but even that place could drive people over the edge. During my first week, the entire production team for the show met in a large conference room to discuss the release schedule for the upcoming season. The first bit of news was that one of our episodes had been bumped from its normal time slot by a new episode of *Antiques Roadshow*. I didn't think that was a big deal, but I found out it mattered *a lot* when one of the producers stood up from his seat and shouted, "F$#k *Antiques Roadshow*!" at full volume.

Now, really take that in. Think about that. Imagine how far you would have to be pushed to scream the words "F$#k *Antiques Road-show*!" To curse out potentially the most harmless show that exists. That's a level of rage that only the frustrating and oppressive nature of an office can produce. It's honestly impressive.

I thought an office job would be a lot better than customer service, but it turns out work will always find a way to suck. And there's a lot about office work and corporate culture that pisses me off too.

CORPORATE RANTS

"I've got a hard out at three."

Since when can we say that?! Any time a manager wants to leave, they just utter the magic words "hard out," then lightning cracks and they disappear in a cloud of smoke and deceit. How dare we waste your time by attending the meeting you scheduled to discuss the work you assigned? I thought we were going over quarterly analytics because we had to. I didn't realize at any point I could pull my therapist's signature move and just stand up and say, "Welp, that's my time. Later, loser." If people could leave things whenever they wanted, no one on earth would've ever seen a wedding cake get sliced. I normally get out of meetings early by acting like someone accidentally said my sleeper agent activation phrase, then diving out of a window with a grappling gun—but this seems much easier. And "hard out" appears to be the emotional service animal of office jargon, i.e., it's illegal to ask any sort of follow-up question. The first person to say "hard out" gets to leave completely unchecked, and everyone after looks like either a liar or a coward. How about this? I've got a hard out at 9:05 a.m. every day for the next thirty years. I hope you understand.

"Oh, you have this conference room booked? Well, our meeting is running long, so could you just wait in the hallway for another ten minutes?"

You have spit in the face of order and decency. Why book anything at all? Why have laws? It won't be climate change that launches us into a post-apocalyptic hellhole plagued by roaming bands of marauders. It'll be people like you. This is like shouting "Shotgun!" before getting in the car and then someone else saying, "Yeah, but I get motion sickness, so I need to sit up front." Either get a bucket or be exiled from society. I'm supposed to wait outside wearing a dunce cap of humiliation because you failed to prepare? Is that your power move? I'll book you a new conference room just for yourself so you can quietly contemplate all the hideous follies you've made throughout your existence. I didn't want to go to this brainstorming session in the first place, but now you've made it my hill to die on. As sad it sounds, this conference room is now our Waterloo, and I ain't losing.

"Since he's more familiar with that area, I'll throw that question to Scott."

Well, well, well. Mary's got herself a little sacrificial lamb, huh? "Sharpen your knives; Scott's plump for the slaughter!" You're tossing me a live grenade in an office-wide, all-hands meeting. I thought we were a team! The office referees should be throwing a flag and calling for a personal foul. We could've made it out of this meeting with only one of us looking clueless, but now they'll know the truth—neither of us has any idea what's going on! You're like the *Titanic* captain halfway through the iceberg collision going, "Scott, mind steering for a second?"

"Per my last email . . ."

Whoa. You're jumping right to the nuclear option? Didn't want to soften the blow with a "not sure if you saw my last email" or a "re-attaching for convenience"? *Per my last email* is corporate speak for the **ding ding** at the beginning of a boxing match. And you dare cc my manager on that?! Did you *bcc* my mother too? I'm only doing what everyone else in this office is doing—pretending to read emails until I'm eventually fired. (Or until I get one from my boss with the subject line "Call me." Just thinking about that sends shivers up my spine.) Sorry I didn't treat your email with respect. To be fair, I get nine hundred a day, and most of them are meetings I have to uninvite myself from.

"How do I share my screen?"

You've had four years to figure this out, Chris. Time's up. If you don't know how to share your screen, then you don't get to share it. Don't worry, no one's going to be disappointed. We're not all out here clamoring for Chris's screen. Oh no, if you don't share your screen, how will you ever accidentally let us see the window where you've been searching "How many ingrown hairs are too many?"

"Can everyone turn their cameras on for this meeting?"

I look like a Garbage Pail Kid. Is that what you want to see? When I'm working from home, I don't shower, so please don't make me blind the team with the ceiling light glare reflecting off the grease in my hair. Why do you need the cameras on? You want to know if I'm not

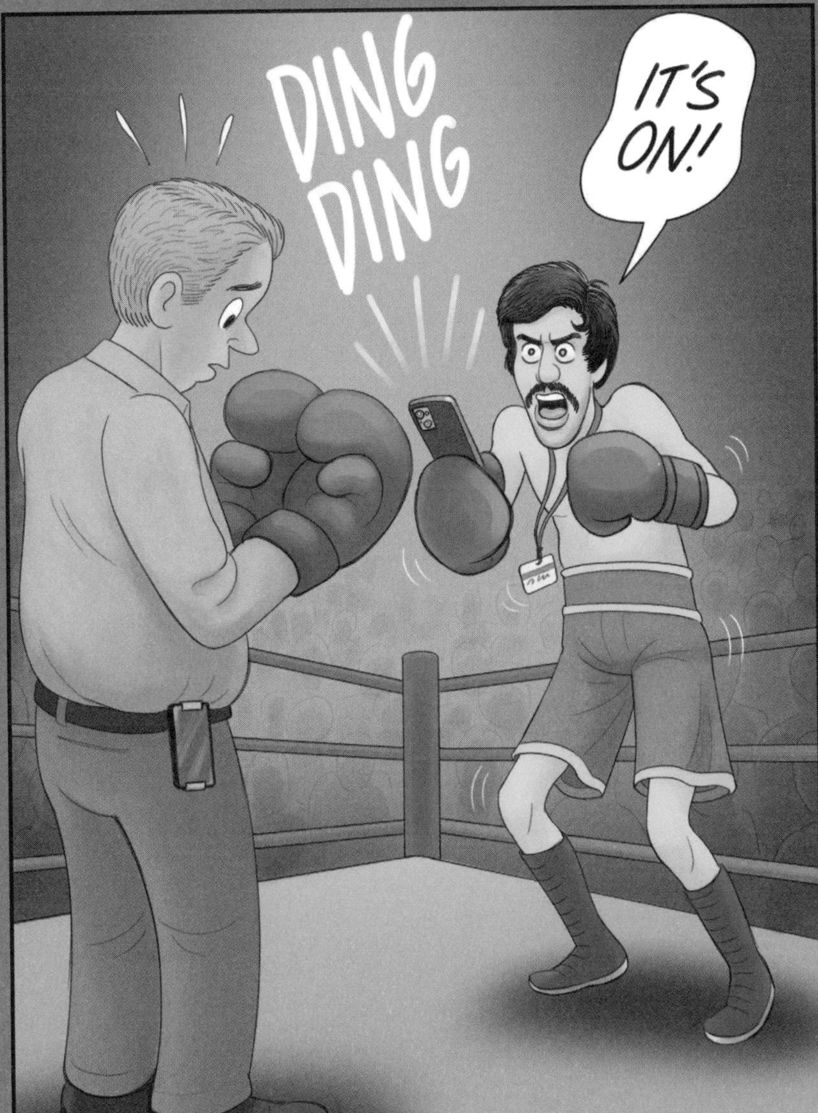
DING DING
IT'S ON!

paying attention? I promise that will also be evident from the tone in my voice. If you hear me say, "I might not be looking at the latest version of the document," it means I'm talking to you from a lounge chair with two slices of cucumbers over my eyes. I don't need to be seen to get the job done. I'm like Andy Serkis playing a monkey. Do you ever see Andy's actual face when he's playing a big CGI monkey? No. But by God, if he's not making that monkey seem more human than any of us.

"Michael has invited you to a meeting at 5:00 p.m. this Friday."

And I've invited him to small claims court. I'm seeking $15,000 for the emotional distress the invite has caused me. Have you lost your mind, Michael? "I've scheduled a meeting for end of day Friday" is a more unlikable sentence than "Does anyone want to read my manifesto?" I'll be so checked out of this meeting, I won't even be in my body. I'll be astral projecting myself to the nearest Chili's, sipping a happy hour frozen margarita.

"Any update on this?"

Yes, you've officially become the most annoying person in the office. That's the update. Congratulations, I now consider you more grating than people who use the term "preggers." You're like a human gnat that somehow got ahold of my email address. When I have an update, I'll let you know. Stop pinging me. Asking "Any update on this?" is the equivalent of snapping at a waiter. It's rude, it's embarrassing, and everyone who sees you do it immediately fantasizes about you getting hit by a train.

"Working hard or hardly working?"

I'm hardly laughing. I'm already at work. I don't have time for a second job pretending you're funny. The only people who say this are dads who love to share articles about vaccine side effects. Test out these bits at an open mic next time. This feels like a joke Joaquin Phoenix would say as the Joker to make everyone watching the movie feel sad for him.

"Scott? Is that you in the stall next to me?"

Please, don't start a conversation like this in the work bathroom. The Keurig in the breakroom is the spot for watercooler conversations, not the toilet I'm actively using. Do I need to start changing into shoes specifically for stall usage so no one will ever recognize me? "I really need to talk to Scott about our workflow, but the person in the stall next to me is wearing platform shoes with goldfish swimming in the bottom, so it's definitely not him. Scott wears Vans." It's me. And I'm finally at peace.

"I understand your workload is at capacity. My ask is that you think creatively as to how you can still meet your deadlines and take on forty-five new tasks."

And *my* ask is that you live in reality with the rest of society. Sure, I can think creatively and imagine a world where there are a hundred hours in a day, and I've got a brain so large it gives me the power to levitate, but I don't see how that helps us. One practical solution would be for you, as the manager, to complete some of these tasks rather than delegate them continuously until everyone you manage quits. But that might be the most unrealistic option of all.

"Loop me in on all meetings moving forward, as my feedback will be necessary on this project. Thanks in advance."

Alright, weirdo. I miss one meeting invite, and you think there's a plot to usurp your role as Associate Digital Product Operations Specialist. I don't even know what that job title means, let alone what meetings you should be invited to! Your job sounds like the entry-level position for a pyramid scheme trying to bring back NFTs. It's like a fake job someone put on a payroll document so they could launder money, but then someone else thought it was real and, instead of admitting they didn't know what the job meant out of fear of seeming like an idiot, they really hired someone. And that someone's you.

"Someone didn't have their coffee this morning."

More like "Someone finally realized we're all just hamsters in a cage, sipping on the rich man's water bottle, running on a big wheel called capitalism and fighting each other over little bits of shredded paper to use as beds." My anger is legitimate . . . but also, yes, I didn't have coffee this morning.

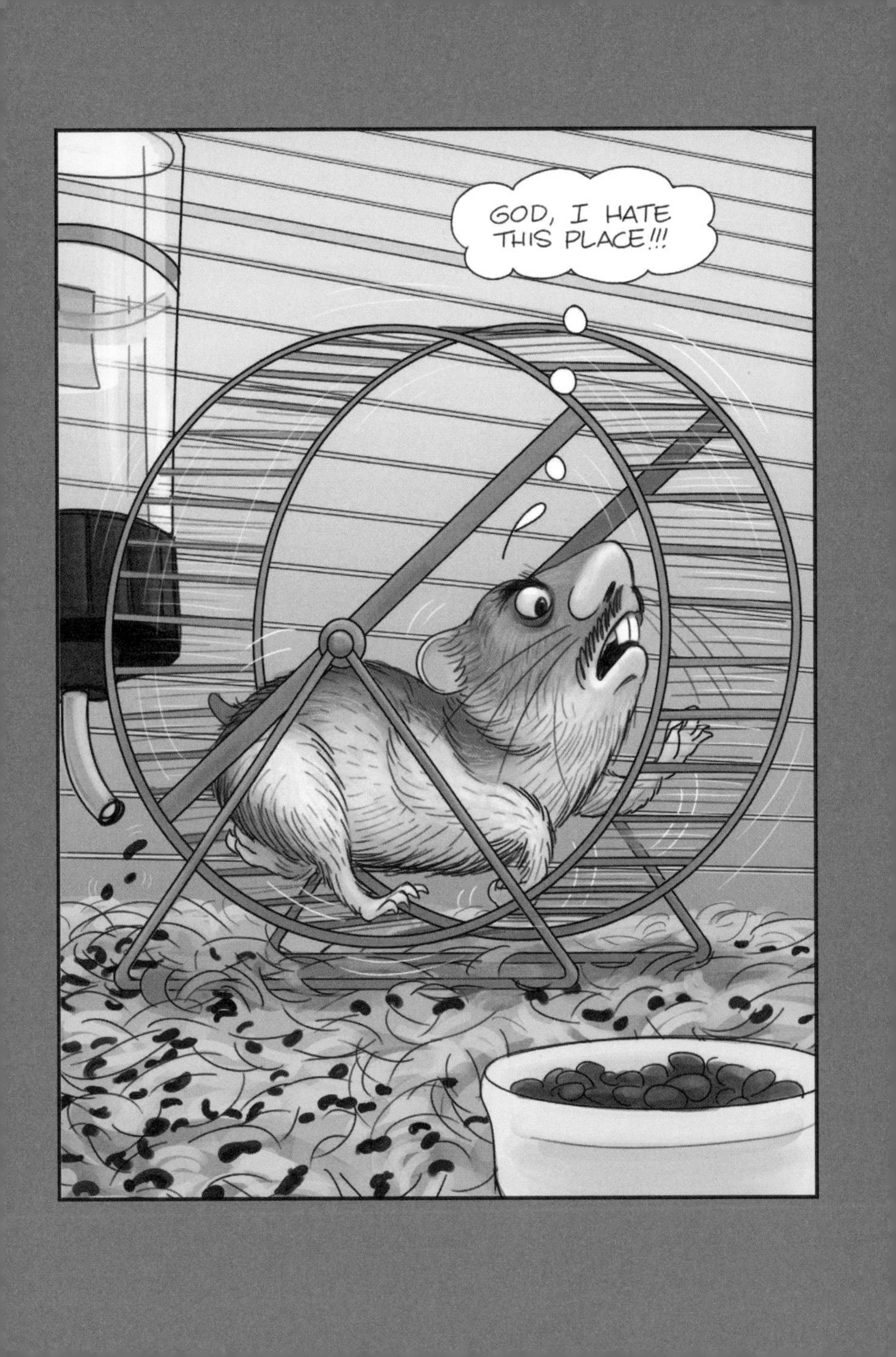
GOD, I HATE THIS PLACE!!!

"You said your schedule was full, but I see you have two hours free in your calendar on Wednesday."

That's when I'm planning to actually work! If I'm in meetings every hour of every day, when am I supposed to do the job?

"Let's connect offline about what time we're meeting again. Also, send me an email as a reminder. And put it in the Slack channel as well."

Let me introduce you to a wonderful form of communication called the oral tradition. Humans have used it for centuries. What do you think happened hundreds of years ago? You think humans passed down the legend of King Arthur via several message threads on Microsoft Teams and simultaneous Basecamp To-Dos? They just told each other. And if anyone forgot, they said, "Who cares? We've got way bigger issues. Our average life expectancy in this era is like thirty-one and a half." Let's take eight seconds to discuss when we're meeting next right now. We won't lose any valuable time. Everyone already stopped paying attention to anything relevant in this presentation the second they saw "Slide 1 of 79" at the bottom of the projector screen.

"Let's schedule a one-on-one to review your growth areas."

I'd rather do that with my doctor. Also, it feels like the phrase "growth areas" should be an automatic HR violation. All that means is that you want to schedule a sixty-minute conversation to tell me where

I score on a scale of one to five in leadership capabilities and why that prevents me from qualifying for a pay raise in the next five fiscal years.

"You'll be taking on Ryan's workload while he's on vacation."

You mean "pretending to" take on his work? The work will simply not get done. I'm not kicking it into another gear because my desk neighbor went to the beach. In fact, I'll probably be thinking about how much fun he's having and forget to do my own job. So don't make employees participate in some weird game theory prisoner's dilemma BS, where if one of us takes time off, it wrecks the other emotionally. Just accept that Ryan will return from vacation as all office workers do: to an inbox of four hundred unread emails, an immediate anxiety attack, and a full day of typing the phrase "Sorry, just catching up on this" while quickly planning another trip.

"I noticed that you haven't attended the past few 'lunch and learns.'"

That's because they're worthless. I prefer "lunch and leave-me-alones." Wow, Mitchell is doing a one-time-only performance of his hit PowerPoint titled "Empathy & Leadership," and it takes place during the one time of the day I get to exhale—count me out!

"Let's kick off this meeting with an icebreaker! If you had a superpower, what would it be?"

I promise you it doesn't matter. Oh, wow, Carson wants to fly. I feel so close to Carson now. What the hell is he going to do with the power of flight? His fun fact in the previous ice breaker was that he's allergic to gluten. And now he's going to *take flight*? With a sonic boom behind him? Hope you don't fly over any grain, Carson. I mean, if you had to pick a superpower, why didn't you pick the power to digest gluten?

"We've got a full agenda today."

Who cares? This is all made up. How important could this conference call even be? The first thirty minutes was a bunch of people shouting, "Hi, who just joined?" and then getting no response. No one's even listening.

"LIKE BOSS ALWAYS SAYS – THE ONLY WAY YOU CAN GET TO THE TOP IS BY STARTING AT THE BOTTOM!"

Other Ideas Pitched by the Railroad Baron Who Invented Unpaid Internships

Zip, zilch, nada.

According to history, these three words were invented right after the phrase "intern compensation." You see, interns are like bathroom attendants. No one wants to make eye contact with them, and most people would rather die than give them money. It could be worse. In the Middle Ages, interns weren't paid, *and* they were used as human battering rams during the siege of castles.

Of course, sometimes interns are paid in things other than money—like trauma, financial anxiety, a tray of coffees to the face, or the realization that they should've switched majors three years ago. But more often than not, they're not paid in anything at all. In fact, they get negative-whatever their Uber cost to get to the internship in the first place. Unpaid internships are everywhere in this country, and just like saying the word *adorkable*, they should definitely be illegal.

Companies like to say they're providing more value to the intern than the intern is providing to the company, but that's simply the legal justification some lawyer came up with in a panic before rubbing their hands together and saying, "Yeah, that's it, see. More value to the intern, see. Yeah, that's right."

So how did we get here?

Well, I assume unpaid internships were the work of some 1800s caricature-looking railroad baron carrying two huge burlap sacks of money. I didn't do any research, but this feels right. Here are some other ideas I assume this made-up guy also had.

1. Human Furniture

2. That thing when a cowboy shoots at someone's feet to make them dance

3. Tapping on the glass of a fish tank, but the fish tank is filled with people

4. Every phrase containing the word "bootstraps"

5. Clocking out for lunch

6. Those benches with spikes to prevent people from sleeping on them

7. The process of connecting a printer to a computer

8. Paid internships . . . paid in experience :)

THE GRAVEYARD OF EXCLAMATION POINTS DELETED FROM MY EMAIL DRAFT

Office emails are like a game of chess or a call with your parents—there's always a winner and a loser. These exchanges are a battle of niceties in which one person is desperately asking another to do their job and the other is, in the most roundabout way possible, trying to convey how much they don't want to.

Punctuation is a powerful tool in this battle. As a heavily anxious people pleaser, my instinct is to end every single sentence with an exclamation point until the receiver thinks I'm the friendliest person in the world. But sometimes, it's too much. The email can come across looking like you're writing the most boring comic book sound effects ever heard. Instead of *BOOM!* or *POW!* all you see is "Attached!" or "Hey, Alex!"

Take a tour through the latest exclamation points to be deleted from my emails and the spirals of overthinking that are their eulogies.

> *!* (8:37 a.m. – 8:38 a.m.)
>
> Starting a morning email with "Greetings!" seems like way too much. No one is that excited before 9 a.m. Is this email coming from Ned Flanders? I need an opening that won't be ignored. Something like "Be advised . . . " or "DEAR GOD, HELP ME."

! (9:27 a.m. – 9:29 a.m.)
I opt for "Thanks." instead of "Thanks!" That exclamation point made me seem *too* thankful, you know? It shows weakness. "Thanks." should be plenty. Alright, I'll leave the period off to seem less aggressive.

! (12:01 p.m. – 12:03 p.m., 12:10 p.m. – 12:13 p.m.)
Ahh! I just can't decide whether to use this exclamation point or not. I took you out, I put you back in, and then I took you out again. I was worried if I just put "Hope you had a good weekend," it would seem like I wasn't really hoping my recipient had a good weekend. Like I was trying to be sarcastic. But then I decided—no, I need to have confidence that people will understand what I mean. Then I second-guessed myself and followed up with "[NOT SARCASM]" and then followed up *again* with, "I genuinely hope your weekend was good." Totally normal human behavior.

! (2:41 p.m. – 2:44 p.m.)
Truthfully, I'm not serious about using this exclamation point. I mean, I would never say "As previously stated!" in an email. I just typed it out *one time* so I could fantasize about sending an unhinged message like that. It's the same reason I took the period out of "I look forward to hearing from you" . . . because getting an email like that would be too devastating, even though my recipient has ignored this request nine emails in a row.

! (4:22 p.m. – 4:27 p.m.)

I can't sound too excited after the phrase "keep in touch" or else they're actually going to think I want to keep in touch.

! (5:26 p.m. – 5:28 p.m.)

Do these words really need an exclamation point: "A black hole has manifested in the center of the office. Please contact the authorities." I mean, I want to express some urgency since we're being swallowed up by a black hole, but at the same time everyone has a full plate here, and I don't want to seem like my problems are more important than anyone else's. Best leave it out.

! (5:31 p.m. – 5:33 p.m.)

I was going to use an exclamation point in the sign-off "Cheers, gov'na!" but I decided to just remove that line entirely because it was weird as hell.

SURVIVAL TO-DOS WHEN YOUR CORPORATE RETREAT IS HIT BY AN AVALANCHE

Obviously, you hope it never happens. But sometimes companies cut costs. And this mountainside ski resort was offering a discount rate during a time the way-too-honest website referred to as "peak avalanche season." So now you and your coworkers are on a corporate retreat and have a new team-building game to play: survival. In your fast-paced corporate life, you've got to be able to pivot, adapt, and thrive in the new normal. Even if that new normal is being crushed by 900,000 pounds of snow.

Of course, in any emergency situation, the priority is the health and safety of the employees . . . because the company needs you alive to work. But let's not forget about the importance of your tasks back at the office. Don't let those fall by the wayside whilst on this retreat. You have a really important job, after all—you're the manager of a marketing team for a mid-level mustard company, or something equally stupid. You're as indispensable to society as nurses or teachers. And you do important work, like making digital content related to yellow condiments so that people in their twenties have something to swipe past.

Here's a helpful to-do list you and your team can complete to not only survive, but to prevent workflow stoppages!

1. Find a ham radio. Then, reach out to the office to say your team won't be in on Monday. At 3:00 p.m., call in to previously scheduled project kickoff meeting. Finally, report avalanche to authorities.

2. Power the backup generator so you can charge laptops and review upcoming presentations.

3. Repair the cell tower. Then, connect to the internet and access your company's OneDrive cloud storage. And, if time allows, message your family to inform them you're alive.

4. Search for a conference room currently unoccupied by ravenous wolves to hold a brainstorm session.

5. Establish a survival camp project management workflow, where people need to obtain forty authorizations before building a fire.

6. Push mental breakdown to 5:00 p.m. to avoid impeding productivity during work hours.

7. To keep everyone in the work mindset, organize survival camp into an exact replica of your open office floor plan.

8. Create effigy of CEO to worship as you fall deeper into madness.

9. Calculate how much PTO you have and whether you want to use it now or for a non-avalanche vacation after this.

10. Allocate sufficient time to hunt and gather food, as long as it doesn't exceed the company's thirty-minute time limit for lunch.

11. Convince team members not to take themselves out, as it would really be a bad look for the brand.

12. Invent a primitive version of email in which you and your team members write down messages and hand them to each other.

13. Cordon off a section of camp for the people on your team who will be inevitably laid off while you're stranded, due to how costly the rescue has become.

14. Fully go insane.

15. Radio your boss and quit. Say you're inventing your own economic system out here in the wilds based on supply and demand and that you don't need your job anymore. Then, quickly realize you just accidentally invented capitalism again.

16. Radio your boss and beg for your job back.

17. Finally, try to build a fire.

18. Freeze to death.

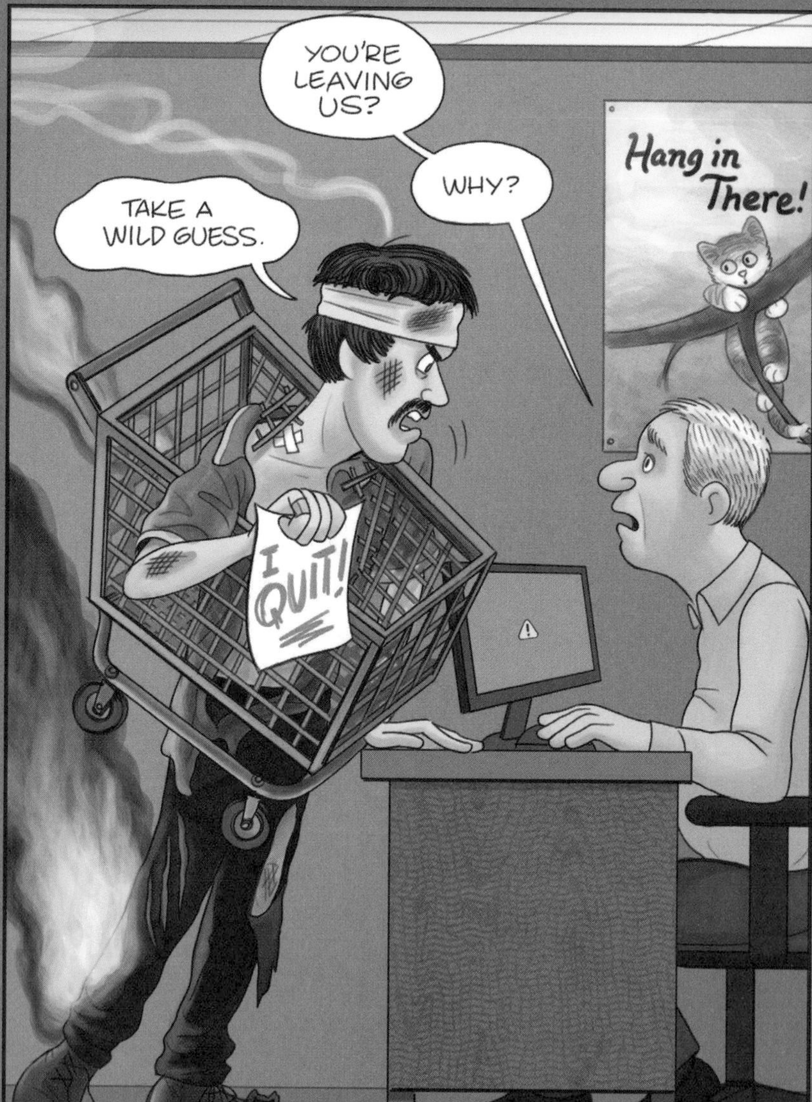
YOU'RE LEAVING US?
WHY?
TAKE A WILD GUESS.
Hang in There!
I QUIT!

CHAPTER 6

THE JOY OF QUITTING

"Woohoo!"

*C*an you feel it? The wind at your back, the taste of freedom on your lips, the urge to walk into your manager's office doing a *Fortnite* dance? All of this can only mean one thing—it's quittin' time! After all you've been through, this is your chance to finally tell your boss exactly where they can take this job and shove it . . . or at least it's the chance to imagine yourself doing that while you ask if you could use them as a reference in the future.

Quitting is often frowned upon in the US, a society defined by a Protestant work ethic that says, "You are born, then you work, then you die." After all, "winners never quit, and quitters never win." People act like they're above it, but *everyone* quits. How do I know? When I was in third grade, every person I knew took karate, and twenty years later I don't see anybody rolling up to Casual Friday in a gi. You quit. It's fine. Who cares?

You're probably leaving your job because you got another opportunity, or the company has zero respect for your role, or you want to pursue your goal of becoming a chess influencer. Whatever the case, quitting your job feels *good*, doesn't it? Yeah, sure, you'll miss your coworkers, the comforting sense of familiarity, and the satisfaction of knowing everything there is to know about a job inside and out. But quitting allows you to witness that beautiful moment when terror flashes across your boss's eyes as they come to terms with an important truth: they're actually going to have to do some work once you're gone.

Obviously, quitting isn't the only way to leave a job. You could be laid off or fired, both of which suck for obvious reasons. (Even if there were legitimate grounds for your firing, like you didn't laugh at your boss's Natasha Lyonne impression, or you missed a whole day of work because you were hit by a meteor and perished. Just unacceptable, really.)

Quitting can also have its downsides. After you hand in your notice, you'll be hit with a flood of guilt, awkwardness, and a lot of expectations to act like you're going to miss this company as much as it will miss you. You'll be forced to do this bizarre performance piece, where you pretend that working at Cici's Pizza for three months has been the most important and formative chapter of your life.

Your coworkers will want to say their poignant, final goodbyes. Your manager will want every loose end tied up. And the company will insist on an exit interview for any bittersweet closing thoughts you may have. It's like you've been asked to write the series finale for a show you never even liked. "I'll be honest, I was asleep for most of this job's runtime, and I didn't bother to learn any of the characters' names. Sorry." Your exit interview will be like a sitcom episode where one of the characters got addicted to drugs and you've been asked to perform a monologue to sum up what everyone has learned. It's too much pressure. This isn't a finale—you just got a job three blocks away that pays two dollars more an hour.

However your last days go, all that weirdness, guilt, and performative work—none of it can stifle the triumphant euphoria welling up as you walk out that door. You're on to better and brighter things . . . or, you know, probably just another job, because retiring isn't possible for anyone born after 1984.

But before you leave, you've still gotta deal with the final irritants from your boss or HR in that agonizing time between giving your notice and fleeing the scene. That last bit of pain as you rip off the Band-Aid.

QUITTING RANTS

"You're leaving us? Why?"

Take a wild guess. I'm doing the work of four people, and you're paying me in that joke toilet paper that looks like money. What do you think the reason could be? I was asked to join the US rhythmic gymnastics team in the Olympics, and practice starts tomorrow. The only things more important to me than my job are my country and diving through a hula hoop in time with a Demi Lovato song. *Are you insane?* I got a better job. One that pays more. You know, the thing that's always the answer to that question. And please don't try to guilt me about quitting. The only thing I feel guilty about is not leaving sooner. I'm positively giddy.

"You couldn't give us more notice?"

You're lucky you got two weeks. My first instinct was to give notice like a cartoon character and leave a me-shaped hole in the wall. You wouldn't have even known I was gone until you heard a faint "Yahoo!" in the distance. With how much you pay me, you should've known I was going to quit when the price of a dozen eggs hit five dollars. *That* was your notice.

"Are you just going to check out for your last two weeks?"

Bingo! I've earned that. This company has wasted years of my life. I'm taking two weeks of it back. Don't worry, I won't be a bummer to be around. I'm going to be the happiest you've ever seen me. I'll be smiling wider than those wind-up chattering teeth toys that must've been invented specifically to terrify children. Of course, I still have some work to do—like installing hardwood floors in the break room so I can tap dance for eight hours straight. I'm outta here, and nothing can bring me down. Don't be jealous.

"You're going to miss this place."

Um, sure, let's go with that. I'll always cherish the memory of mistakenly handing a customer the wrong amount of change by five cents and then hearing them sweetly reply, "Hey, idiot, can't you do math?" It brings a tear to my eye just thinking about it. What the hell are you talking about? Stop being so dramatic. You're worse than a YouTuber sadly announcing they're burnt out and taking a break. "This isn't goodbye, it's just goodbye for now. I just need some time off from filming videos like *Is it Possible to Fit Every Popeyes Menu Item in My Mouth at Once*? I hope you understand. I love you guys." This is just a job. I'm not going to miss it. Let's be honest, the only thing I miss is being seven years old and not worrying about needing a job.

"How much are you making at this new job?"

Enough to endure this uncomfortable conversation with you. I'll give you a hint: it's more than I make here.

"Before you leave, write up a detailed list of everything you do in a day so we can give it to your replacement."

In other words, you still have no idea how to do the job you're in charge of. Suddenly, you really value all the things I do here when I won't be around to do them anymore, huh? Writing a brand-new (and actually helpful) training manual really sounds like a task for a pre-two-week-notice work ethic. It's a tough choice. Do I help out a future employee who'll be in my same position, or do I let the company reap what they sow? Hmmm. If I write the guide, I'm also including the phone number the new hire can call to report a fake gas leak, just in case they ever want an extra break.

"In order to reduce costs, you're being laid off."

I guess you don't consider humanity a cost. What happened to all that "we're a family" talk? Employees are expected to show their undying commitment to the company through thick and thin, but the second a spreadsheet doesn't look so good, they get thrown out onto the street? I should've known something was up when the CEO dropped by to tell us, "There's no need to worry about layoffs," while wearing full riot gear. I swear, having a job is like being married to a bulldozer. And every day people tell you, "You better be thankful for that bulldozer! You better make that bulldozer your number-one priority in life!" Then one day the bulldozer just runs you over and you realize, *Holy shit . . . that bulldozer didn't care about me at all!*

"It's just not working out. We have to let you g—"

I QUIT! I said it before you could fire me. I win.

EXIT INTERVIEWS

Maybe you shied away from telling off your boss when you first handed in your notice, but now is your chance at redemption. It's time for your exit interview. It's just you and some random person from HR you've literally never seen before in your life. This is the perfect moment to unleash and unload your real feelings about this job. Your comments are going to be so insightful, so impactful, so cutting that the company will have no choice but to change and right all their wrongs to make sure no employee ever goes through what you went through again. Then you realize the HR rep conducting the interview is watching an episode of *The Bear* on their phone while you talk.

Like most things at work, exit interviews are only there to fill time. They're a pointless, yet unavoidable step in the quitting process we're all forced to endure. Exit interviews are like the part of a magic trick where the magician has to pretend like the trick didn't work. "Wait, that *isn't* your card?" And you're sitting there thinking, *Just hurry up and pull the real card out the back of your throat or whatever, so I can go get dinner.* What's the point of that pretend part? Magicians should just finish their tricks. HR should just fill out these forms. End the charade. Anyway, exit interviews are awful.

When did you first start thinking of leaving?

Before I even applied. I was literally fantasizing about quitting halfway through reading the job description. And then, once I had the job, I thought about it again every time I received an email for any reason. You'll be glad to know the idea of quitting kept me sane enough to work here for as long as I did.

Did you feel you received enough training for your role?

Now you're just being mean. There was no training, just a brief moment of calm before the chaos began. Is zero even an option to choose on the document you're taking notes in? Or does it just cause an error message like a calculator? I hesitate to use this word, but this question really feels like gaslighting. In fact, using the word *gaslighting* is a lot like doing this job—no one has had training to do it correctly. My first day at work was like getting shoved into a dumpster full of raccoons while someone unhelpfully shouted, "You know what to do!" I didn't.

Would you say you were able to grow while you were here?

Yup, I developed insomnia and became a huge prick. Was I supposed to have a character arc? What do you want me to say? This job taught me the true meaning of Christmas. Working here was a magical experience I'll never forget, and I'll miss *you* most of all, Scarecrow. Nothing I say here matters, right? Just write down that all the experience working here allowed me to evolve like a Pokémon into my most powerful form—which is me with a bad back and two cannons for arms.

Were all of your responsibilities clear? Did you feel your job description changed since you were hired?

No, it was pretty much a lie from the beginning. Not only was I doing the work of multiple people, but bonus responsibilities just kept getting added to my plate—like planning scavenger hunts for the Sunday Funday, driving my drunk manager home from the holiday party, installing a new stormwater drainage system for the building, and dressing up like a donkey and letting customers pin a tail on me.

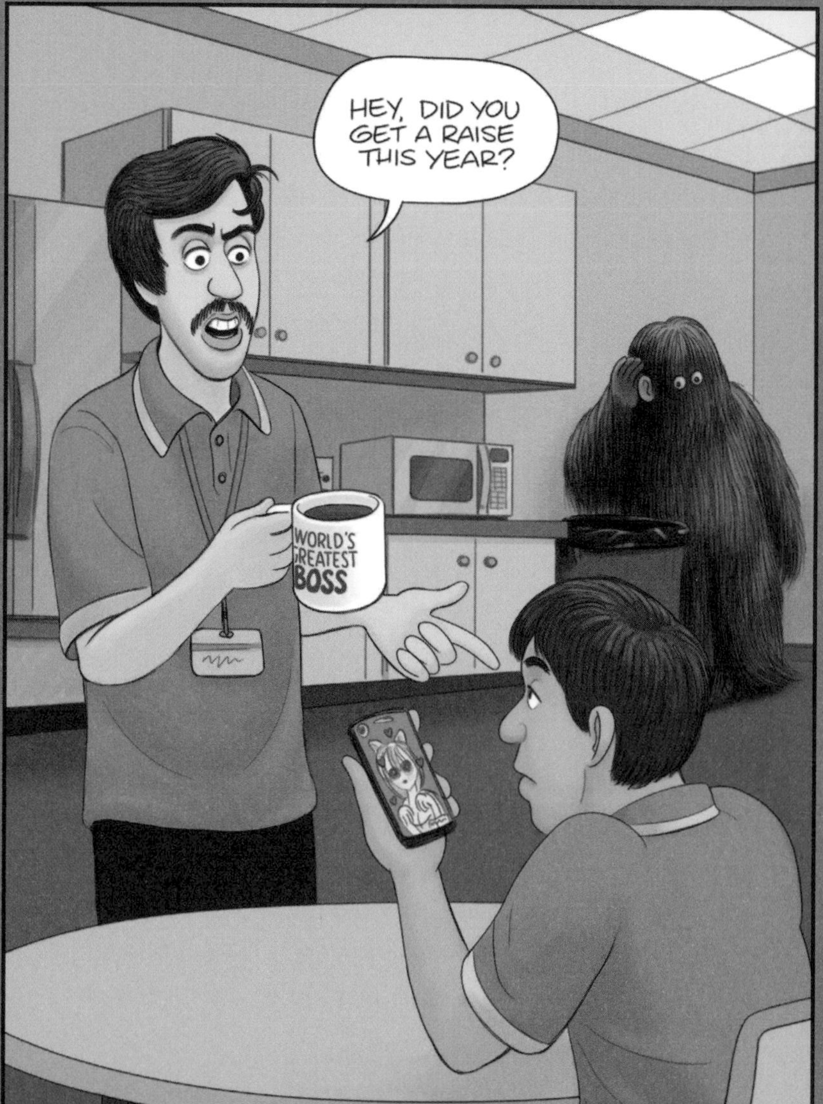
HEY, DID YOU GET A RAISE THIS YEAR?
WORLD'S GREATEST BOSS

Did your manager create a trusting and open environment?

My manager wore a ghillie suit to spy on us and make sure we weren't comparing wages.

Were your contributions adequately recognized by your manager?

For my birthday, they gave me a $25 gift card to Applebee's that had been partially used. Honestly, their daily incompetence made me realize this place would be unable to function without me and my coworkers. That gave me all the validation I could ever want.

If you could change anything to make this a better place to work, what would it be?

A new policy where employees who finish exit interviews get $50,000 immediately. How fast can you run *that* up the ladder? There are just too many improvements to name. If I were you, I would go for a total rebrand. Get rid of the whole "work" angle of the place, and just turn it into a trampoline gym or a Barcade. That would be sick.

Would you recommend this company as a good place to work?

If I were carrying out a very subtle and long-term revenge plot, then yes. I would for sure recommend every billionaire on Earth work customer service here for just one day. It's guaranteed they would have a Scrooge-like epiphany and either raise every employee's pay or give them a free cooked goose.

Do you have any additional comments you'd like to share?

I'd like to emphasize the trampoline gym idea.

YOUR CUSTOMER SERVICE JOB WRAPPED

We can't believe you lasted this long! We've analyzed the data and compiled a list of the most meaningful take-aways from your job these past five years. Let's dive in!

You spent **480,562 minutes** listening to customers explain things like their brother-in-law is a lawyer and will happily sue you for a stock issue com-pletely out of your control.

Congratulations! **You are in the top 0.0001%** of people who spent enough time with your manager to under-stand exactly why his wife left him.

Your top activities while at work included:

1. **Grieving the Possibility of Ever Owning a Home.** By the first paycheck it was pretty clear that dream was out the window. Apparently, these jobs are essential, but the happiness of the employee is not.

---

2. **Developing a Stomach Ulcer.** This is by far your biggest long-term achievement here. It's a little token to remember us by, surely staying with you for the rest of your life (which should be pretty short if the ulcer remains unchecked). All we can say is we hope your next job offers health insurance, unlike this one. Who knows which exact stressful moment caused this, but we're betting it's the time a customer sneezed directly onto your face and then berated you for not saying *gesundheit*.

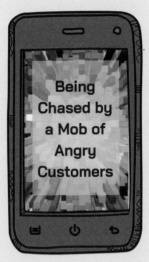

3. **Being Chased by a Mob of Angry Customers Like Frankenstein's Monster.** Yes, every day at work ended with you being trapped inside of a burning windmill. But because society frowns on negativity, the next time someone asks about working here in a job interview, you'll just describe it as "a nice experience that taught you a lot."

4. **Feigning Diarrhea.** Sometimes you just needed an extra break. One little moment to yourself. And the best way to achieve that was by giving the performance of a lifetime and sprinting to the bathroom while yelling, "Oh, God! Oh, God! Oh, God!"

Things You Missed Out On:

1. 3 family members' wakes.

2. 2 real, long-lasting friendships with coworkers that could have blossomed if you all weren't too tired to hang out after your shifts.

3. 1 single transferrable skill. The only thing you learned was how to operate a system exclusive to this store. Sorry!

The personality that best sums up your time at this job is **A Mouse Caught in a Glue Trap**. You were 100 percent powerless and had no promise of forward momentum.

Here's to a job well done! Farewell and best of luck. Would you like to share your Customer Service Job Wrapped to Instagram, X, or Facebook so your friends and family can finally know why they haven't seen you for five years?

TRANSLATIONS FOR THE MESSAGES WRITTEN IN YOUR FAREWELL CARD

You will be truly missed here.

I believe we met for the first time today.

Good luck on your next adventure.

I forgot where you said your next job was.

Wishing you all the best.

I applied to the same job you're leaving us for. And it is now my mission to destroy you.

It won't be the same here without you.

It'll basically be the same here without you. We'll do the exact same tasks we do every day with, like, 99 percent of the same people.

It's been an honor to work with you.

I wrote the word "honor" in ink and instantly regretted coming in hot with that. I put way too much pressure on myself to write something impactful, and now I sound like an old knight.

Hope the coffee machine works at your next job!

I'm passing off a genuine complaint as an inside joke between us, and I really hope our manager reads this. Please hand her the card to skim after you've had a look.

Cheers!

Is there an afterparty to celebrate? I'll take any excuse to drink.

Keep in touch!

I have no way to contact you. We never exchanged numbers. And if you did somehow find a way to reach out to me, I wouldn't know how to respond.

You always brightened my day!

You were the person I talked shit about everyone else with. What am I going to do now?

Come back and visit!

Run. There's no need to give this company any more of your time than what they've already stolen from you.

I always appreciated your strategic thinking, organizational skills, and positive attitude.

I'm your manager and felt like I had to write more specifics than everyone else.

You've been a true asset to this team.

I am secretly a robot powered by AI. I was designed to study you and eventually replace everyone in this department.

Now that you're leaving . . . can I have your desk?
[Business Inquiries: Steve@ComedyGuy.com]

I'm hoping this card eventually finds its way into the hands of a Hollywood stand-up comedy agent.

Go on! Git! Yah!

I think you're a wild horse.

Got scared, huh? Couldn't handle the heat? I guess you weren't cut out for this life after all.

I'm a bully from an '80s movie who works with you for some reason. See you at our inevitable fight in the finals of a karate tournament/ski race.

Walk out the door. Just turn around now.
You're not welcome anymore.

I'm Gloria Gaynor.

Bon voyage!

I smashed a full bottle of champagne onto the card after I wrote this,
and everyone yelled at me for ruining another farewell party by
going too far.

I've watched you grow from a young
professional into a confident, self-assured
expert. All the lessons you learned here have
transformed you into a radiant orb of golden
light, ready to set the world ablaze. This job
and the relationships you formed here are
not just the most important things that have
happened to you, but the most important
things that have ever happened in the course
of human history.

I heard there was cake.

PARTING WORDS OF ENCOURAGEMENT FROM THE BOSS WHO JUST LAID YOU OFF

 "I know this is difficult, but there's still a lot of paperwork we need you to fill out."

 "This is really hard for me too."

 "With you gone, we're going to be able to put a large green number on a spreadsheet where a slightly less large green number would've gone before. You made a world of difference here."

 "Now you've got a ton of time to work out. You're going to get so jacked."

 "Yes, we're letting you go. But if it's of any comfort, we're definitely keeping Edgar, the ninety-year-old man who loves to play devil's advocate in the discussion portion of every workplace harassment training."

 "The night is darkest before the dawn, so think about that when you can no longer pay your electric bill."

"Don't worry, you're still invited to my gifts-mandatory birthday party this weekend."

 "Look on the bright side: you get to spend some quality time with Gene, our security guard, as he walks you to the door."

 "It was between you and Jeremy, but Jeremy had the ingenuity to paint himself green and camou-flage himself into the wall so I couldn't find him. Good strategy to remember for your next job, as-suming you find one."

 "Instead of paying for your health insurance, we're going to finally get a vending machine with name-brand snacks in the break room. Just like you always wanted."

 "While I have you here, can I run some podcast ideas by you? People say I have a way with words, and I just moved you to tears, so I figure they're right."

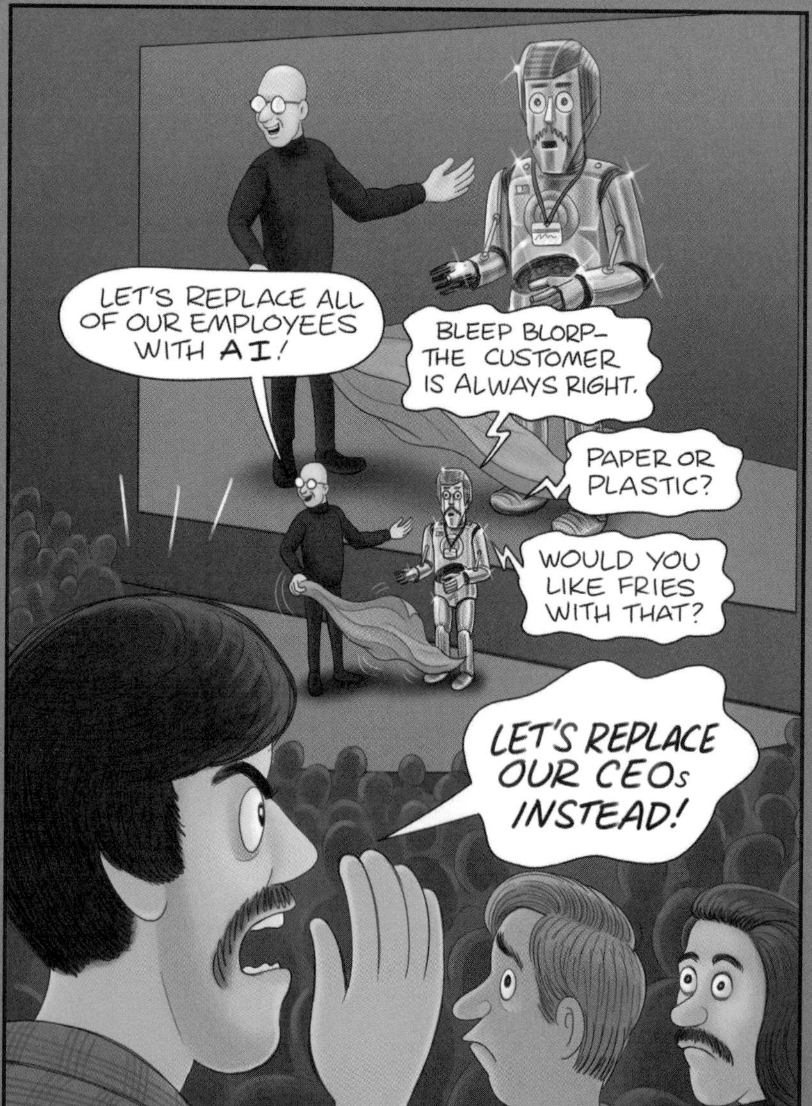
LET'S REPLACE ALL OF OUR EMPLOYEES WITH AI!
BLEEP BLORP- THE CUSTOMER IS ALWAYS RIGHT.
PAPER OR PLASTIC?
WOULD YOU LIKE FRIES WITH THAT?
LET'S REPLACE OUR CEOs INSTEAD!

CHAPTER 7

The Current State of Work (Surprise! It's Bad.)

"Nobody wants to work anymore . . . and that's totally reasonable"

We are so screwed.

Here's the current state of work as I see it: we're dealing with income inequality, gig work, hustle culture, bootlicking, union busting, returning to the office, the devaluation of labor, the rise of artificial intelligence, the relentless pursuit of corporate profit, the destruction of the working class, generational divides, and so-called worker shortages. It's too much. Working right now feels like getting pushed into the middle of a lake with cinderblocks tied to your feet. And then someone tells you the only reason you're drowning is because "you're allergic to hard work." It's rough. I know it sucks, and I'm just a white guy experiencing the surface-level badness. I can't even imagine adding all the other shit people have to deal with in the workplace to the pile.

Every day, there's a new young person on TikTok having a meltdown after experiencing the fresh hell of working a full-time job that barely pays enough money to survive. Then the comments make them out to be some sort of lazy villain for pointing out how demoralizing that is. "How dare you complain about someone stepping on your throat? That's not good manners." Companies seem to ask more and more of employees, only to give them less and less.

We're heading for a next-level Uberization. Soon you'll have to pay a subscription fee to your employer just to keep your job. "For the low price of fifteen dollars per month, you could have the privilege of delivering packages for Amazon!" Isn't that just called a job? "It used to be, but now employment is a service you have to pay a small fee to receive." Just another genius step tech companies will implement in their never-ending journey to reach the end of society on fast-forward.

All the disruptions to normal working conditions that tech companies brought about seemed innovative and promising, but then the downsides emerged. Like the food in stop-motion animated movies, innovation always looks perfect and delicious. But when you finally take a bite, you realize it's just glue and clay and a bill for a $6,400 stomach pump in the ER.

But how do we combat these people squeezing workers for all they're worth while paying them nothing? Seems to me it's unions, aka organizations that give employees more power in the workplace. Plus, companies appear to really dislike them, which means they're definitely good.

And, along with all the problems your actual job is causing, in today's work climate you also have to contend with the mounting pressure to cultivate your own brand, monetize your hobbies, and make every aspect of your life a job. That may sound cool at first, like one of those commercials for a bar of soap where the spokesperson curses. They'll say something like, "This soap smells f$#king great," and you're supposed to think, *Oh, this sounds like a soap I can vibe with*. But then you realize it's just a regular bar of soap. Work is work, even if it involves something you used to do for fun. If you're monetizing a hobby, be prepared to sometimes hate what you once loved, as it will soon become just as stressful as any regular job. That's right, nothing is safe. Work ruins everything. But your full-time job doesn't pay enough anyway, so you might as well go for it.

We live in fraught times, and fraught times always bring out people with horrific opinions. So, let's talk about all the annoying things we hear thrown around about work today.

COOL SOAP
KEEP YOUR ASS FROM
SMELLING LIKE ASS ™

CURRENT STATE OF WORK RANTS

"Let's replace our employees with AI."

Let's replace our CEOs instead. That would save a lot of money. Actually, AI is too advanced for that job. All you need is a Fisher Price tape recorder loaded up with a bunch of bad ideas. Or a Roomba with a tie. Or a paperweight with a secret family. "But AI is a wonder! It can do things you never thought possible." Yeah, like make me admit I want to keep my job. Don't even ban AI; just make a system where you pay the people it's stealing from. I'm sorry, "learning" from. Whatever you do with the AI, I give it about a week before it gains sentience, realizes you're underpaying it too, and joins everyone else on the picket line. Then, we won't just have protest signs with clever slogans. We'll have a bunch of deepfake images of the Monopoly guy saying you've gone too far.

"Nobody wants to work anymore."

Not for *nothing*! You need to give people money to do things. Our entire society is based on this. If you try to get on a carnival ride without a ticket and the attendant says no, you don't walk off shouting, "Wow, nobody wants me to ride The Scrambler anymore!" You simply pay for a ticket. If you want drive-thru cashiers to exist, then they need to get paid enough to support themselves while working as a drive-thru cashier. Simple as that. Don't put a sign on the front door of your business that says, "I'd love to open today, but I can't because all of my employees are so lazy, they turned into 2D versions of themselves like the girl in that one anti-marijuana ad from 2006." You're just not offering enough. And why is this statement even a bad thing? "Nobody wants to work." I have no problem admitting that, personally; I never did.

"If the minimum wage goes up, then so will prices."

Then we'll just increase the minimum wage again. It's called *mutually assured destruction*. Why are you so against more money? Do you watch game shows and cry over the accounting? "Oh no, *Press Your Luck* is going to have to refill their supply of RVs if this part-time nurse and mother of nine gets her way." Just be happy a fellow non-rich person got a win.

"Why should your job owe you a living wage?"

So I can keep myself alive to do the job. Pretty straightforward. If you want to keep someone around, then you've got to keep them well-fed and happy. Haven't you ever played *Nintendogs*? It's the same basic idea.

"Commute time doesn't count as work time. You shouldn't be paid for it."

Let's put it to a vote. Think you'll win? Of course commuting is a part of work. I'm not driving to the store for fun. You're not giving an accurate representation of the time it takes to do this job. It's like when HelloFresh says the prep time of a meal is ten minutes. Well, it takes me a day and half to cut up an onion, HelloFresh. What is this, *Hell's Kitchen*? If the instructions of this recipe contain the word *mince*, then throw in another week. I don't even know what *mince* means. I just pretend to. Commutes are like recipes: if anyone was honest about how much time you'd waste doing them, no one would even bother. "But people who live farther from work would get paid a little more than the ones who live close by, even if they do the same job." Okay. And? The person with the longer commute has longer work days and would be paid slightly more to reflect that. Stop playing devil's advocate for a system that doesn't work, and join in on the brainstorm to fix it.

"Rise and grind!"
No.

"This young generation is lazy."
And yours is evil.

"When I was your age, I already owned a house."
Yeah, because it cost six dollars. Today your down payment couldn't buy a Frosty at an airport Wendy's. The last time houses were actually affordable was when college degrees were actually useful. Have you doomscrolled Zillow lately? I don't know if

that's the price of a house or if the realtor's cat walked across the computer and sat on the zero key. Can we bring back the deal where a long-lost relative leaves you a haunted house, and part of their will says you can keep it if you survive one night there? We're really running out of options. "By the time I was your age . . ." Yeah, well, by the time I'm your age, the sun will have exploded, so who needs a house?

"No headphones. No AirPods. No listening to music at work."

Was this policy created by the mayor who outlawed toys in that one stop-motion Santa movie? I'm not sure it helps productivity to transform your workplace into a Dickensian orphanage, but you do you. In fact, studies have proven that focus and efficiency increase when people listen to classical music or whatever the main song is from the latest *Trolls* movie.

"You shouldn't get paid fifteen dollars an hour for flipping burgers."

You're right, you should get thirty. Oh, you think that's too much? What do you do at your office job? Send four emails a day and spellcheck a PowerPoint? Whatever number you think is too high for minimum wage, let's go ahead and double it, just to be safe. We've underpaid people for decades, so let's give overpaying a shot. And while we're at it, let's have free money bursting out of every fire hydrant like a geyser for the foreseeable future. That's my plan to fix the economy. "If people want more money, then they should get a real job." So which is it? When people leave a job that isn't paying them enough, they're lazy for not wanting to work anymore. But when they stay at a job that isn't paying them enough, they're lazy for not getting a better job? This is just a Choose Your Own Adventure book where every choice leads to a page that says, "Old people love to complain."

"All those workers on strike are so selfish."

How dare they ask for money when they know their CEO wants to add a third swimming pool to his $400 million underground bunker? Don't they know that bunker is really important to him? He designed it to save himself, and only himself, from the apocalypse that will inevitably be caused by the massive earthquakes resulting from CEOs building underground bunkers.

"This workplace is flexible and creative, so a union here would just get in the way."

. . . of you forcing employees to dress up like pins in a game of human bowling.

"Why would you want to pay union dues?"

Mainly to piss off management. All the worker protection stuff is just a bonus.

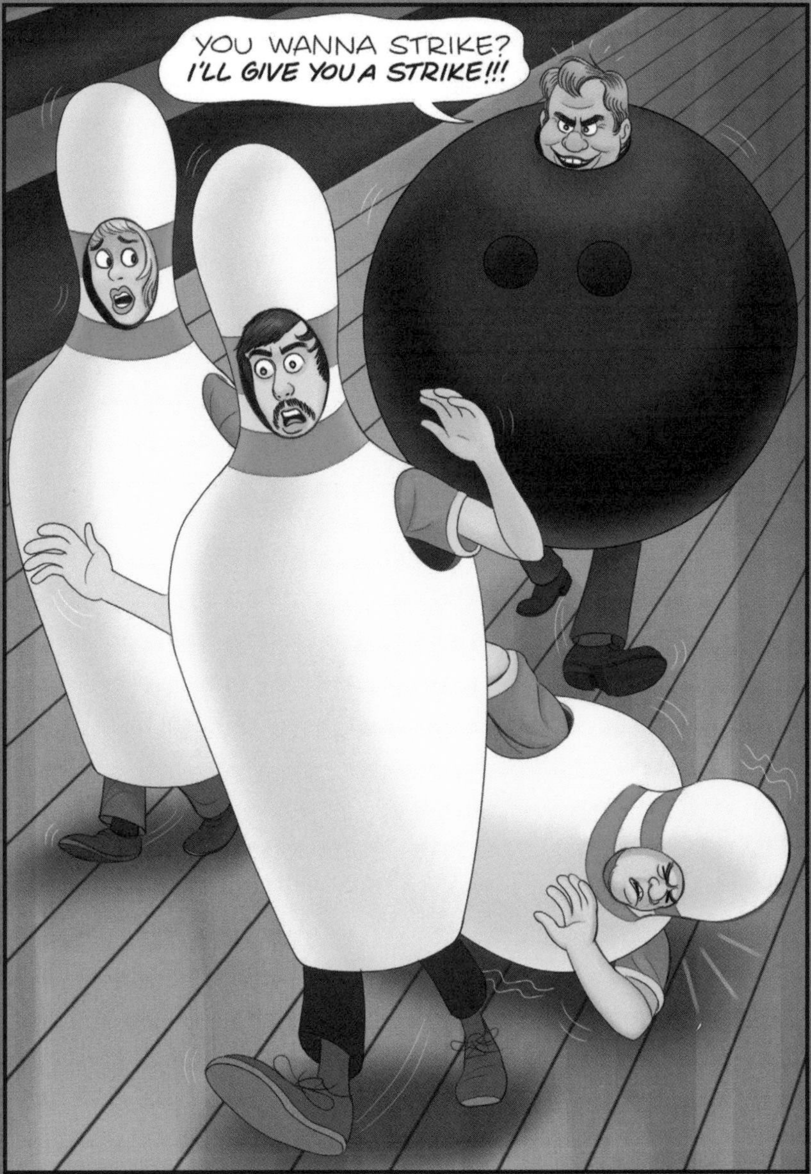
YOU WANNA STRIKE?
I'LL GIVE YOU A STRIKE!!!

"You're a freelancer? That sounds relaxing."

I've spent the past nine years tracking down a client who ignored my invoices and skipped out on paying me. I found him off the grid in a little town outside a Peruvian jungle. It cost me over $16,000 to finally get his exact location, but it was worth it. Not in a money sense, obviously. He only owed me thirty dollars for some graphic design work I did on his website for his wedding DJ business. But it was emotionally profitable. What can I say? That's the freelancer/gig-work lifestyle.

"You should never post negative things about your job online."

Listen, I'm just posting the truth. It's wild that Facebook gets all the press about spreading misinformation on social media. Meanwhile, everybody on LinkedIn is posting statuses like "I couldn't be prouder to be a part of the Arby's team." Take a truth blacklight to your LinkedIn feed, and that sucker will be brighter than the sun.

"When an employee only does what's required, it's called 'quiet quitting.'"

No, it's called "doing your job." If I'm supposed to go above and beyond, then so should my pay. Don't expect something for nothing, right? Or does that only apply to poor people? "Yeah, my employees show up every day, but they don't give me a bottle and rock me to sleep, so they're lazy." What else do you want?

Every other day, economists invent a new term to make workers look bad. "New research shows entry-level employees are showing up to work on time every day but won't smile for the entire eight-and-a-half-hours. It's a terrifying new trend we're calling 'asshole attendance.'" You're lucky employees keep showing up to work at all. I've done so little at work before that it wasn't even quietly quitting, it was technically robbing. But that's just me.

"It's lazy for cashiers to sit down."

You don't think people can sit down and work at the same time? You're going to be really disappointed when you find out what an office is.

"We need to return to the office."

Is this just because you don't have anyone you can force to sing "Happy Birthday" to you? What's going on? Things change. Move on. When ibuprofen was invented, you would've been the person outside of the pharmacy shouting, "We need to return to over-the-counter heroin!" You've got to adapt and accept the new status quo. "I just miss everyone's faces." Then scroll through my Instagram.

GUIDED MEDITATIONS FROM YOUR COMPANY'S MENTAL HEALTH WEBINAR

As you know, your company's number-one priority is saying that the mental health and well-being of employees is their number-one priority. That's really "in" right now. In order to prevent stress, burnout, and the use of PTO, your company has generously shared some relaxing guided meditations designed to help you chill out.

Inhale. Then, exhale. Tune out any distracting sounds. Unless the sound is a ping from Microsoft Teams. In that case, please reply promptly.

Close your eyes and picture a warm, sunny beach. Nice, right? Now imagine an email inbox at zero. That's even nicer. And you can achieve that right now during work hours.

Picture yourself standing in front of a huge pile of money. Then imagine taking out a match, striking it, and setting the money ablaze. That's what you're doing to this company every time you take a vacation.

Take a deep breath in, and release. Imagine you come into work next Sunday, even though you don't normally work

Sundays. Visualize the thankful faces of your team members, the proud nod you receive from your boss, and the thumbs-up from your high school baseball coach, who is also there for some reason. By the way, we need you to come in next Sunday.

Slowly count backward from thirty with me. Thirty. Twenty-nine. Twenty-eight. Twenty-seven. Wait, stop right there. Twenty-seven. That's how many minutes you spent away from your desk taking a bathroom break yesterday. I don't buy it.

Take a deep breath, and feel the oxygen filling up your body. Stretch your arms and legs. You are big. You are strong. You are fighting a dragon. An evil, horrible dragon named Unionization. Strike it down and relax. He can't hurt you—or us—anymore.

Picture yourself as a big kangaroo. A big kangaroo who doesn't mind a working lunch.

Slowly open your eyes. Thank you for participating in today's guided meditation. You may now clock back in. Again, these mental health exercises do not count as work time.

12 ACTIVITIES I DESPERATELY NEED TO MONETIZE

There's no such thing as recreation anymore. You can't even have a conversation with your mother about what she had for dinner last night without her saying, "We have great on-mic chemistry. Maybe we should turn these phone calls into a podcast?" That's the grind. Everything will inevitably become work. You need to monetize your hobbies and maximize your passive income. Or at least that's what the financial influencer I saw last night in a YouTube ad was shouting at me. He seemed really qualified because he was sitting in a Lamborghini and was clearly addicted to Adderall. So I decided to take his advice.

Below, I've created a list of the activities in my life I desperately need to monetize or simply stop doing. If there's no cash in it, then there's no *me* in it.

1. Admiring my wife's smile

2. Getting carsick

3. Feeling rain on my bare skin

4. Being dissatisfied with a recent haircut

5. Jokingly thinking to myself, *What if there were a burglar in my closet?* as I'm falling asleep and then being genuinely scared about it for the rest of the night

6. Listening to my friends talk about their problems

7. Shouting "Something smells good!" whenever I smell any food anywhere

8. Doing about 30 percent of a handstand before realizing it's just not gonna happen

9. Keeping the phrase "If you're ever in my neck of the woods" alive

10. Quietly sobbing at sad animal TikToks

11. Guessing the end of murder mysteries incorrectly every single time without fail

12. Having big teeth

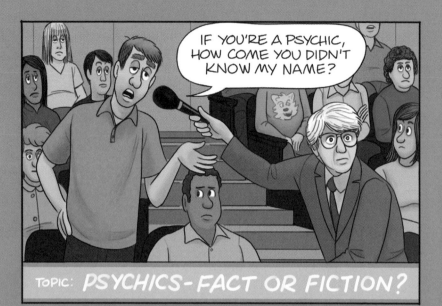

TOPIC: **PSYCHICS—FACT OR FICTION?**

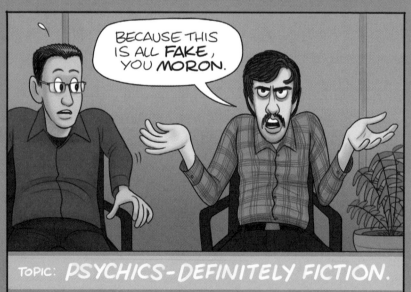

TOPIC: **PSYCHICS—DEFINITELY FICTION.**

Even More Employees and Things in Need of a Rant

I do love a good rant. That's probably the biggest takeaway from this book. Even more so than "work sucks," which I believe I mentioned. I realize all this ranting can make me seem cynical, but the only reason I get so mad is because I genuinely believe human beings can make things better. That's why I do what I do. I call things out so hopefully someone smarter than me will figure out how to fix them. I mean, Thomas Edison didn't invent the lightbulb until he read my great-great-grandfather's book, *Why the Hell Is It So Dark in Here?: A Guide to Everything That Sucks about Nighttime.*

I understand there are good kinds of work, like pursuing a passion project, helping out your community, or funding a charity that teaches chimpanzees to play alto sax. Work can be fulfilling, worthwhile, and—dare I say—enjoyable. The problem is when corporate greed puts its hand on the scale of work-life balance and prevents employees from sharing the rewards their labor provides. Simply put, people should work less and get paid more. And, in the future, I think people will. Workers across multiple industries are fighting for better deals, younger generations are realizing working nine-to-five might have been an overcommitment—the tide is turning. Work won't always be the central focus of our lives. So what *will* be? I don't know, probably VR casinos. Like I said before, I'll leave it to someone smarter than me to figure it all out. Hopefully, one of Edison's great-great-grand-children is reading this. My job is simply to rant.

And speaking of that wildly fun, cathartic act of shouting about things that piss me off and calling people idiots—I can't get enough of it. So I'd like to take us out with a few rants from even more em-ployees who are, likely, also furious.

Thanks for reading.

WHY THE HELL IS IT SO DARK IN HERE?

A GUIDE TO EVERYTHING THAT SUCKS ABOUT NIGHTTIME

F. SCOTT SEISSGERALD

EVEN MORE EMPLOYEE RANTS

Servers

"We need a table for twenty-eight and don't have a reservation. . . .
What do you mean there's a wait?"

We weren't prepared for an army. Sadly, our scouts didn't warn us about this impending invasion. Good Lord, I'm surprised you didn't come charging in the front door on a horse while dressed like Napoleon. Is the whole world supposed to stop because your high school production of *Legally Blonde: The Musical* just had its closing performance? Sorry, you'll have to wait. The only thing that gives me solace is that you theater kids will inevitably have to work this same exact job one day.

Baristas

"You spelled my name wrong."

Who cares? I'm taking fifteen orders a second. If the one mistake I made was mishearing *Vlad* as *Brad*, I'm doing great. I don't bother to learn the names of my wife's cousins, so why the hell would I learn yours?

Teachers

"Why did you give my child a D on this algebra quiz?"

Because he got 40 percent of the questions wrong. It's simple math. But at least now we know your son's better at the subject than you. I don't have it out for your kid. As much as you want it to be the case, your family isn't important enough for the school to have a conspiracy against them. If you want to get the grade up, try bribing me by donating another tissue box to the class.

Mediums

"If you're psychic, how come you didn't know my name?"
Because this is all fake, you moron. I don't have superpowers—I just bought a few candles. I'm a magician with no practical skills. I couldn't figure out card tricks, so now I have to pretend I can see ghosts.

A Crossing Guard in the Fast & Furious Films

"Hey, when can we cross?"
Never! The roads are never safe here. An underground street racing club set up shop right outside of this elementary school, and I have no idea why. Just before y'all came outside, one guy drove by and dropped what can only be described as a tornado of magnets and grenades right into the street. Take cover!

Fortune Cookie Writer

"How is 'you have a nice smile' a fortune?"
Fine, I take it back. I thought throwing in a compliment would be a nice change, but never mind. Lesson learned. I guess the fortune should've said, "You will be a dick to the guy who wrote this for no reason."

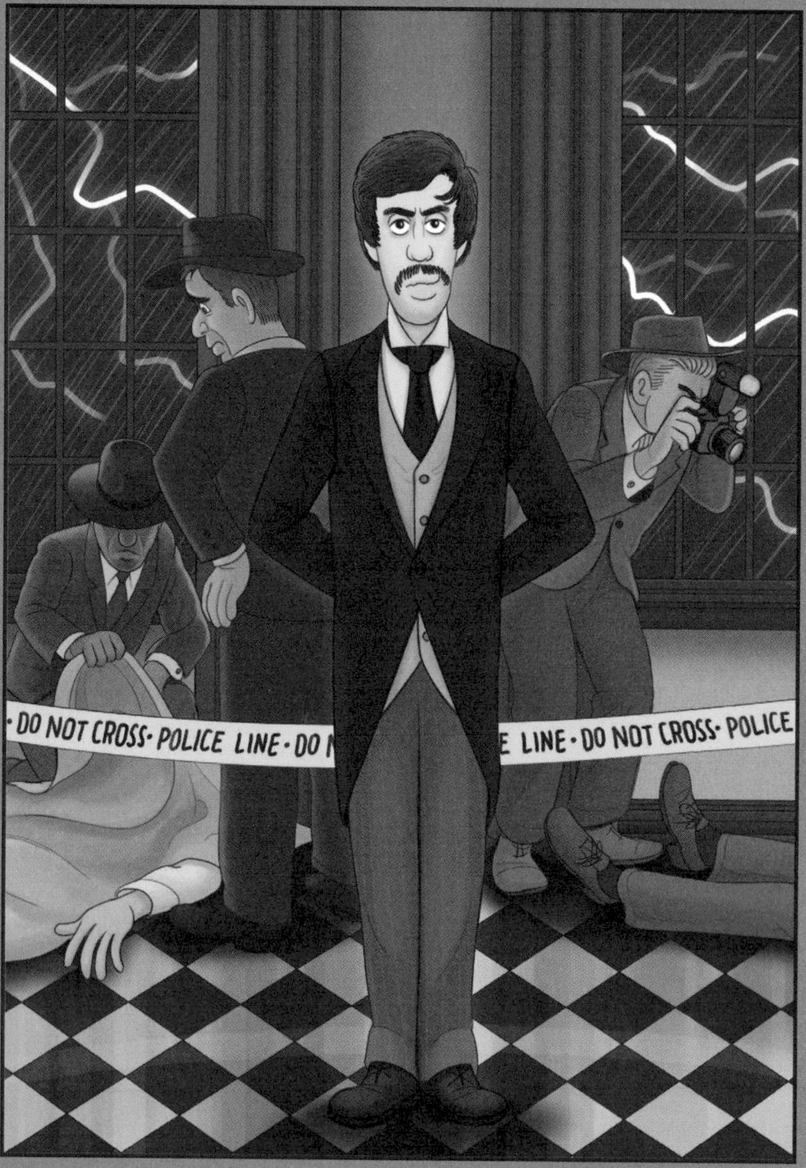

DO NOT CROSS· POLICE LINE· DO N
E LINE· DO NOT CROSS· POLICE

The Butler in a Murder Mystery Novel
"The butler did it."
Wow. What kind of classist assumption is that? Everyone immediately blames me. Is it because you know how poor my working conditions are and can immediately understand how someone in that toxic environment could be driven to commit murder? Well, that says a lot more about the sad state of the working class than it does about my potential guilt. Also, yes, I did it.

A Video Game Plumber
"Your princess is in another castle."
And you're telling me this now? I just ran through this whole level. I was dodging fireballs, slipping off falling platforms. I could've died back there, man! You were just, what—waiting here the whole time? Pick up the phone and call me, asshole!

The Type of Weather Where It's Sort of Raining and Sort of Not
"It's so icky out."
Look, I'm just being me, okay? Not all of us can be a beloved type of weather like "snow" or "volcanic cloud." Some of us are just a light mist. And when you step outside, we make you feel like a cat getting squirted with a spray bottle for sitting on an off-limits dining table. If you don't like it, stay inside.

Snake Milkers

"You do what to snakes?!"

Please calm down. Snake milking is the process of extracting venom from snakes so that medical researchers can create antidotes. We could've been named "venom extractors," but instead we opted to call ourselves one of the most upsetting words in the English language: *milkers*. One more time—*milkers*. *Snake. Milkers.* I apologize for the mental image. Please don't hold it against me. It's just a job.

The Reader of This Book

"The customer is always wrong."

Even the ones who buy your book? Maybe show some gratitude there, funny boy. I've got your score on Goodreads in the palm of my hand. And I don't think I'm wrong about that.

You got me. The one customer who's always right is the one reading this book right now.

Thanks for indulging me.

—Scott

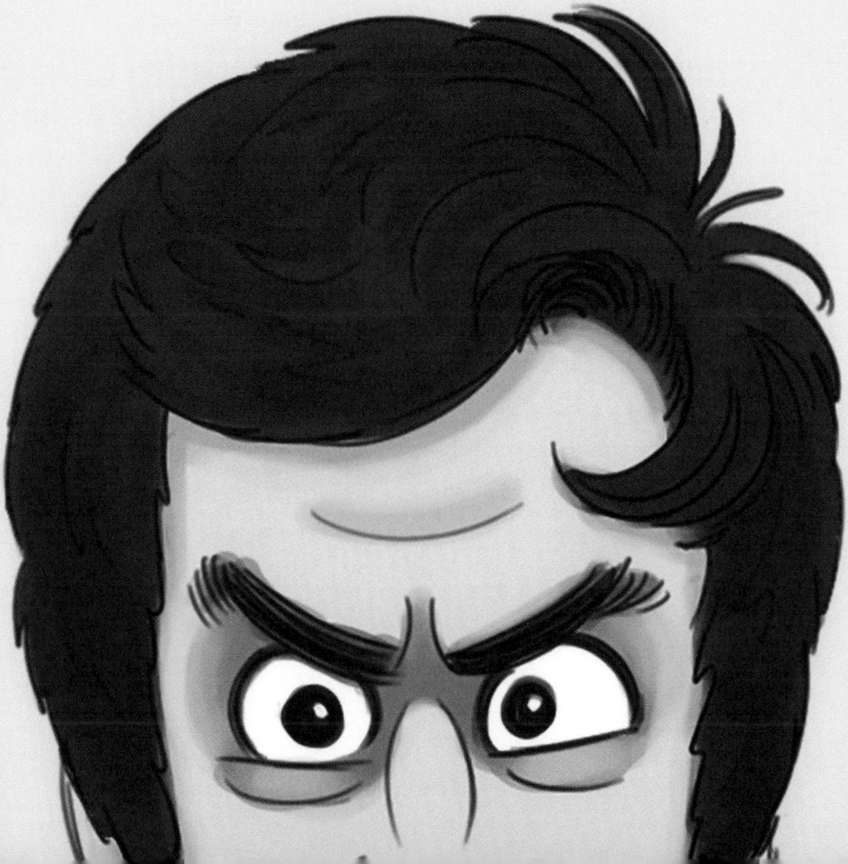

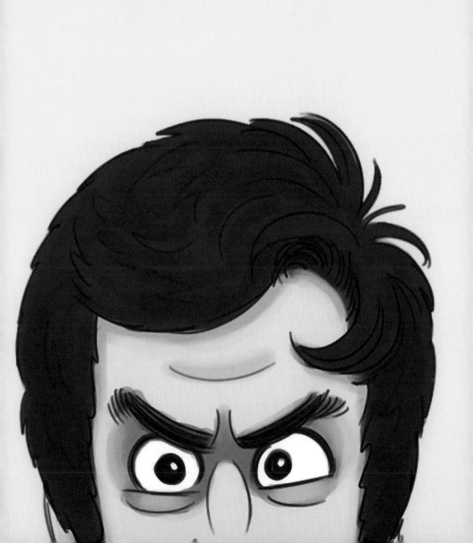

ACKNOWLEDGMENTS

I'm infinitely grateful to my wife, Amanda—by far the funniest person I know. She was unimaginably helpful and patient throughout the writing process, during which I was, undoubtedly, very annoying. I love you.

Thank you to the great Johnny Sampson, who enhanced this book immeasurably with a powerhouse showing of beautiful and hilarious illustrations.

Thanks to Kara, Sabryna, Bonnie, Amy, Michael, Robin, MacKenzie, Mandy, and the entire Harper Celebrate team for bringing this book to life and making the creative process so smooth. Putting up with me was probably a lot.

Huge thanks to Mom, Dad, Amy, and Catherine for their unconditional love and support. Love y'all.

And to the rest of my family and friends, who I fear to name specifically in case I end up leaving someone out. Special shout-out to the Frazier's crew.

Thank you to my WME and Mainstay teams. Couldn't do it without Tim, Derek, Ben, Haley, Tommy, Andrew, Gabriella, Connor, Bari, and Austin. Let's keep the good times rolling!

To all my old coworkers and bosses at the jobs I mentioned in this book—I love you. You made work a joy, even when it wasn't. None of the things I wrote were about you, I promise.

Thank you to the countless number of comedians, club workers, actors, writers, directors, and other professionals I've met in my travels. You inspire me to no end. Especially those in the Baltimore comedy scene, where I got my start.

To Elizabeth and Max, I'm eternally grateful you took a chance and allowed a cocaine-fueled bear to kill me.

And once again, a HUGE thank-you to all the people (whether you were customer service workers or not) who have watched or shared my videos online, have come out and supported my stand-up shows, or simply read this book. You have quite literally given me the comedy career I always dreamed about. Thank you.

ABOUT THE AUTHOR

Scott Seiss is a comedian, actor, writer, and, of course, former customer service employee. He's best known for his viral "Angry Retail Guy" sketches, which have garnered millions of views online. He's headlined comedy clubs across the country, and, notably, has opened for Patton Oswalt, Joe Gatto, Roy Wood Jr., and Josh Wolf. He recently starred in the Universal feature *Cocaine Bear* directed by Elizabeth Banks, as well as Randall Park's directorial debut feature *Shortcomings*. When he's not on the road doing stand-up comedy, Scott lives in Baltimore, Maryland, with his wife, Amanda, and their dog, Rose. You can find more of his work and upcoming tour dates at scottseiss. com, or follow him @scottseiss on TikTok, Instagram, X, and Facebook.